Mathematical
Quilts
No Sewing Required!

Diana Venters
Elaine Krajenke Ellison

KEY CURRICULUM PRESS
Innovators in Mathematics Education

Editor	Crystal Mills
Editorial Assistant	Jeff Gammon
Production Editors	Deborah Cogan, Jason Luz
Copyeditor	Tom Briggs
Production Manager	Diana Jean Parks
Interior and Cover Design	Kirk Mills
Production and Layout	Ann Rothenbuhler
Technical Illustrations	Crystal Mills, Kirk Mills
Cover Photo	Terry Roueche, Roueche Photography
Publisher	Steven Rasmussen
Editorial Director	John Bergez

Key Curriculum Press
1150 65th Street
Emeryville, CA 94608
510-595-7000
editorial@keypress.com
http://www.keypress.com

Printed in the United States of America   10 9 8 7 6 5   06 05 04 03 02   ISBN 1-55953-317-X

About the Authors

Diana Venters

Diana Venters was born in Chicago, Illinois. She attended the University of Illinois, majoring in English with a minor in mathematics. She received an M.A. in mathematics education from Louisiana Tech University and an Ed.D. in curriculum and instruction (mathematics education) from the University of Tennessee–Knoxville.

Diana taught mathematics for 25 years, in seven states, at the elementary, junior high, and high school levels. She has taught developmental mathematics, statistics, and teacher education at the college level since 1988. She is presently a visiting assistant professor of mathematics at Winthrop University in Rock Hill, South Carolina.

Diana has been quilting since 1986. She started making quilts based on mathematical designs in 1988. She and Elaine have been showing their quilts at NCTM conferences, both regional and national, since 1992.

Diana is married to Dennis Venters, a chemical industry consultant, and has three grown children, Steven, Donna, and Laura.

Elaine Krajenke Ellison

Elaine Krajenke Ellison was born and raised in Grosse Pointe Farms, Michigan. She received a B.A. in mathematics from Michigan State University, an M.A. in education from the University of Colorado, and an Ed.S. in administration from Central Michigan University.

Elaine has taught in junior high school, and for the past 14 years she has been teaching at West Lafayette Senior High School in West Lafayette, Indiana. She teaches mainly high school geometry classes, and she also supervises student teachers and works with prospective student teachers from Purdue University. She enjoys art, music, ballroom dancing, golf, skiing, reading, and, most of all, her three children, Mark Hunter Meier, Tiffany Marie Meier, and Scott Matthew Meier. She started quilting in 1987 when Diana introduced her to the art.

Contents

Designing Your Quilt

The Tiling Quilts

Exploring the Mathematics of the Quilts

Designing Your Quilt

Note to Teachers

The quilts that inspired this book were created by two mathematics teachers who worked together in the mid-1980s and took quilting classes together. As quilters, we became much more aware of the geometry of design elements in our environment and began seeing quilt possibilities in many of the mathematics concepts in texts and journals. As we progressed through our series of mathematical quilts, we learned a great deal about the design process. Because we had no patterns for our quilts, we had to draft the design and solve the many problems that arise in this process involving measurement, color, and the sewing skills needed for construction. As we constructed the quilts, we learned new techniques, and as the series grew, so did our skills. One revelation for us was the value of the design process as a learning tool. Taking on a project and working it through to completion provide invaluable experiences in problem solving. As teachers, we need to give our students more opportunities to engage in the design process. Many of the activities in this book provide such experiences.

Learning Geometry and the van Hiele Levels

The activities in this book will help students improve their visualization skills. In their research on how students learn geometry, Dutch mathematicians Dina van Hiele-Geldof and Pierre van Hiele determined five levels of learning through which students must progress to succeed in geometry. Students achieve the first level, visualization, when they recognize shapes by how they look. Students reach the second level, analysis, when they understand characteristics of a shape based on simple definitions. At this level, students can recognize shapes regardless of their orientation in the plane. Students attain the third level, informal deduction, when they compare relationships among shapes and understand minimal conditions to determine a shape. The fourth level, formal deduction, is the appropriate level for formal geometry courses. The activities in this book provide opportunities for students to work at the second, third, and fourth levels of the van Hiele model. The fifth level, rigor, is not usually part of the high school geometry curriculum.

The van Hiele model is especially applicable for students who have difficulty in a formal geometry course but who are otherwise capable students. According to the van Hiele model, when students have not successfully progressed through the first three levels of geometry, they cannot be successful in formal geometry. Age alone does not determine readiness for the study of formal geometry. Exposure to activities that will move students through the first three levels is required for readiness.

How the Book Is Organized

The quilts in this book were all inspired by mathematical patterns. We hope that these quilts and the related activities will inspire you and your students to explore these patterns and enjoy the beauty we have discovered in the mathematics. The book is divided into thematic sections, each highlighting a series of quilts with similar designs— "The Golden Ratio Quilts," "The Spiral Quilts," "The Right Triangle Quilts," and "The Tiling Quilts." After a short introduction to each theme, students encounter a series of activities that guide them through mathematical concepts related to the quilt designs. Each section includes research activities, technology activities for graphing calculators and computers, and Internet activities. The concluding student activities focus on a description and re-creation of the quilt pattern with an emphasis on the art of the design. A description of how to actually make the quilt is included for those interested in sewing their own quilt. Teacher notes, solutions to activities, and a bibliography conclude each section.

When to Use This Book

Although the activities are especially appropriate for geometry students, they can also give pre- and post-geometry students practice in spatial reasoning. Some of the activities are algebraic in nature and would be appropriate for students in beginning or advanced algebra or even pre-calculus classes. You can use these activities to supplement some topics in the curriculum and to enhance others. The "Designing Your Quilt" activities encourage the use of color, and many can be considered as mathematical art projects. It is important for students to see mathematics in many forms, not simply as problems in a textbook. The quilts and the activities based on them allow students to see mathematics in a new light. Math can indeed be beautiful!

Suggestions for Classroom Use

The activities in this book can be used in various ways in the classroom. Although some of the activities within a section are sequential, most can be used separately. You will find information in the "Teacher Notes" sections relating the activities to particular quilt designs. The "Designing Your Quilt" activities following the mathematics activities can be done before, after, or separately from the other activities. The design activities are suitable for enrichment, extension of classroom learning, or purely recreational mathematics.

Students can work on the activities individually or in groups. You may choose to divide the activities in a section so that different groups work on different quilt designs and the mathematical activities that support these designs. Each group can then make a presentation to the class explaining the mathematics and interpreting the design. The Internet explorations and research topics can be assigned as individual projects, to be presented at mathematics fairs or other school programs. Parents, administrators, community members, other teachers, and students will enjoy this unique method of presenting mathematics.

To Quilt or Not to Quilt

Above all, this is not a quilt-making book, even though we have provided abbreviated instructions for sewing the quilt at the end of each section. For those students who wish to re-create the quilts in a form other than sewing, we suggest colored construction paper or fabric. Students can trace and cut out the shapes and glue the pieces to poster board. Students with access to a dynamic geometry software program such as *The Geometer's Sketchpad*® or a computer drawing program may enjoy creating their designs on a computer. Don't be surprised, however, if an interested group of students, or perhaps even parents, gets excited enough to actually sew one of these quilts.

Diana Venters
Elaine Krajenke Ellison

A Brief History of Quilting Around the World

A quilt is a blanket or covering made of three layers of material. The top layer is usually a fabric design, often made of pieces of fabric joined into squares or stitched down (appliquéd) to create a picture. The back layer is usually a piece of utilitarian cloth, sometimes an old blanket or sheet. Today, the middle layer is usually a fluffy batting made of spun polyester or cotton, but in centuries past, this middle layer could have been leaves, newspapers, fresh wool from a sheep, or cotton right from the field, seeds and all. Old blankets and worn clothing have been discovered as the middle layer of quilts. In any case, we know that the three layers, no matter how lightweight they are, provide insulation against the cold. Quilters and seamstresses throughout history have recognized the insulating value of layers of light fabric.

Many Western cultures, especially those in cold climates, have developed some form of quilted bed or wall covering. In most of these cultures, women filled domestic roles. Through their sewing of clothing and quilts, they found a means to express artistic vision. Even in wealthy households, young women were taught needle arts as a way of making practical but decorative items for the home.

Evidence suggests that quilting was introduced in Europe during the Crusades (A.D. 1100–1300). The lighter armor worn by soldiers consisted of tough quilted jackets topped by chain mesh. During the Middle Ages, appliqué designs were used to decorate banners as an inexpensive alternative to the woven fabric in tapestries. In the fifteenth century, the words *quylt*, *qwilt*, and *twylt* appeared in literature describing appliquéd wall hangings.

This tradition of making fabric wall and bed coverings was brought to colonial America by the early settlers. Because of the scarcity of cloth, women began creating intricate patterns with the leftover scraps from making new clothing and from the less worn scraps of used clothing. Women made items their families needed, but they made them beautiful with color and design.

Women throughout history have used their needlework for both beauty and utility. They have also used their sewing projects to make political statements. During the Civil War, the log cabin quilt was used to send messages to runaway slaves. The square for the log cabin is made from a center square surrounded by strips of fabric. Although this pattern traditionally has a red center square signifying the hearth of the fireplace in the home, during the Civil War, if the center square of a log cabin quilt hanging on a clothesline outside a house was black, the signal to a runaway slave was that this was a "safe" house. The Drunkard's Path quilt, which pictures an erratic curved path design, was displayed by members of the Women's Christian Temperance Union in the early twentieth century as a symbol of their protest against alcohol consumption.

In Florida, the Seminoles have a long tradition of patchwork design, mostly in clothing. Whereas most Native American tribes used animal skins trimmed with braid and beads for clothing, in the hot Florida climate, Seminole women began making intricate cloth designs from fabrics obtained from European traders. It is theorized that the Seminoles learned many of their sewing techniques from runaway slaves whom they harbored during the 1800s. With the advent of the sewing machine in the late 1800s, the Seminole designs became more intricate and included geometric bands around the hems of skirts and jackets.

In Hawaii, missionaries from New England brought fabric and taught the Hawaiians to sew clothing. Although the missionaries encouraged the Hawaiian women to cut fabric into small pieces to create designs, the women preferred to work with large pieces of fabric, creating native flower patterns in appliqué from them. Pennsylvania Dutch missionaries may have taught the Hawaiians their technique of *scherenschnitte,* cutting snowflake-like patterns from a single piece of cloth. Large, whole-cloth designs of fruits and flowers native to Hawaii are evident in these quilt designs.

In Japan, women were attracted to quilted fabrics both for decorative items and for clothing. The Japanese culture emphasizes a love of nature and landscapes, and their artistic designs often focus on balance, proportion, and harmony. The oldest known quilts in Asia date from approximately 100 B.C.–A.D. 200. These early quilts contained cross-hatch quilting (a square grid design) and appliquéd animals. Today's Japanese quilters are adapting designs from other parts of the world to suit their culture. Their quilting designs are often examples of Sashiko, a geometric design stitched on whole cloth.

In warmer climates, women often stitched quilted wall hangings, appliquéing animals, human figures, plants, and landscapes onto fabric. In South America, Chilean women often incorporate political messages in their appliquéd images. In times of oppression, their quilts often pictured persecution and executions. Throughout Central and South America, women in various cultures use their needlework as a means of expressing themselves.

In Africa, warriors wore appliquéd quilts and carried stitched banners that recorded their deeds. In West Africa, strips of fabric, some from old clothing, were stitched together to make new fabric. Pictures of animals were often appliquéd to the cloth. Slaves brought to the United States from Africa often duplicated these methods, and string piecing is a method still used by many African American quilters.

Today, quilting is enjoying a revival of interest. Quilters throughout the world are relearning the methods native to their culture, as well as the techniques and designs of other cultures throughout the world. In the United States, quilters who have emigrated from other countries are teaching their methods while they learn the methods native to the United States. Although quilts are still used as bed coverings, smaller quilts often serve as artistic statements.

Source: Willow Ann Soltow, *Quilting the World Over* (Radnor, PA: Chilton Book Company, 1991).

The Golden Ratio Quilts

THE ITALIAN MATHEMATICIAN LEONARDO DA PISA (1175–1250) studied algebra and the Arabic system of numerals while in Northern Africa. At the time, Europeans used the Roman numeral system, and da Pisa, also known as Fibonacci (son of Bonacci), explained the advantages of the Arabic system of numeration (base 10) over the Roman system (I = 1, V = 5, and so on) in his book *Liber Abaci*. For several centuries, this book was the standard on Arabic numerals and algebra.

One of the mathematical exercises in *Liber Abaci* described the hypothetical birth pattern of rabbits and resulted in the series of numbers 1, 1, 2, 3, 5, 8, 13, 21, 34, ... This sequence has been referred to as the Fibonacci sequence ever since Eduoard Lucas, an eighteenth-century mathematician, gave it that name in his book on recreational mathematics. The pattern for this sequence of numbers is additive. That is, starting with the third term, each successive term is the sum of the two previous terms.

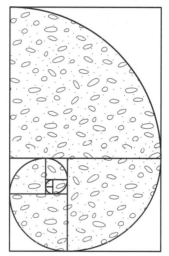

The Fibonacci Sequence and the Golden Rectangle Quilt

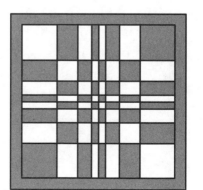

The Fibonacci × 4 Quilt

The Fibonacci × 3 Quilt

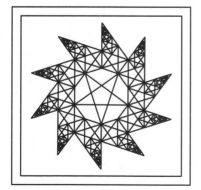

The Lute of Pythagoras Quilt

In the centuries since da Pisa generated this sequence, scientists and mathematicians have discovered that the Fibonacci sequence has many other connections in addition to describing birth patterns. Botanists have discovered that many plants have branching patterns that follow the Fibonacci sequence. The petal pattern of many flowers result in one of the Fibonacci numbers. Economists have used the Fibonacci sequence to illustrate economic cycles. You can also find relationships to this sequence of numbers in Platonic solids, pentagons, decagons, and Penrose tiles, and in the flags of the United Nations building in New York City. There is even a connection between the Fibonacci sequence and Pascal's triangle, as you will discover in the activities.

The Fibonacci sequence is also related to the Golden Ratio. In a Golden Rectangle, the ratio of the length to the width is $\frac{1 + \sqrt{5}}{2} \approx 1.618$, which is called the Golden Ratio. The Golden Ratio is often represented by the Greek letter phi (ϕ). You will explore this relationship in Activity 16: Graphing Calculator Explorations.

Artists, in particular, believe that rectangles whose length-to-width ratio approximates the Golden Ratio are more visually appealing than rectangles whose lengths and widths exhibit other ratios. Some historians believe that ancient architects were aware of this special rectangle and ratio when they designed the Pyramid of Cheops and the Parthenon. Today, many products are packaged in rectangular boxes that feature this ratio to increase the visual appeal to consumers.

Leonardo da Vinci used the Golden Ratio when drawing the human body in a treatise called *De Divina Proportione* by Luca Pacioli. Artists such as Albrecht Dürer, Georges Seurat, Piet Mondrian, Salvador Dali, and George Bellows all used a Golden Rectangle to create dynamic symmetry in some of their works. And Hungarian composer Béla Bartók based the entire structure of his music on the Golden Ratio and the Fibonacci sequence.

There are also many interesting connections between pentagons and the Golden Ratio. The design for the Lute of Pythagoras quilt contains pentagons, pentagrams (a five-pointed star), and decagons. The growth patterns of many organic living forms are based on pentagons, including many flowers, starfish, sand dollars, DNA molecules, apples, and leaflets of tomatoes.

In the activities in this section, you will discover many interesting relationships among Fibonacci numbers, Golden Rectangles, Golden Triangles, the Golden Ratio, pentagons, and pentagrams.

ACTIVITY 1

Fibonacci Rabbits

Fibonacci is often remembered for his hypothetical problem about the breeding patterns of rabbits in his book *Liber Abaci*.

How many pairs of rabbits would you have at the beginning of each month if

   a. you started with a single pair,

   b. each pair reproduced from the second month on,

   c. each pair gave birth to a new pair of rabbits every month, and

   d. no rabbit died?

Mathematical Quilts—No Sewing Required!
©1999 Key Curriculum Press

ACTIVITY 2

The Fibonacci Sequence and Pascal's Triangle

The triangular arrangement of numbers shown here is often called Pascal's triangle. The history of the triangle actually goes back as far as the year 1303, when Chinese mathematician Chu Shih-chieh included it in his work *Precious Mirror of the Four Elements*. In 1653, French mathematician Blaise Pascal wrote a treatise about the triangle, and thus it is usually associated with his name. Copy the triangular pattern shown here, and continue the pattern for seven rows. See if you can find a relationship between the numbers in Pascal's triangle and the Fibonacci sequence. If you get stuck, ask your teacher for a hint.

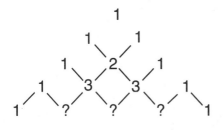

The Fibonacci Sequence and Polygonal Numbers

Mathematicians study many different sets of numbers.
Some interesting number patterns are formed by considering
the geometric pattern of points in a numeration sequence.
For instance, triangular numbers are numbers whose points
can form an equilateral triangle, square numbers can form a
square pattern, pentagonal numbers can form pentagons, and
so on. Draw pictures and find the next three numbers for these
triangular, square, and pentagonal number sequences.

a. Triangular numbers

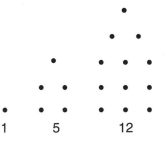

1   3   6

b. Square numbers

1   4   9

c. Pentagonal numbers

1   5   12

The Fibonacci Sequence Makes Connections

Mathematicians are often surprised when one topic they are exploring connects with other mathematical topics, as in the connection between Pascal's triangle and the Fibonacci sequence. Look at your results for Activities 2 and 3, and find as many relationships or connections as you can among the triangular, square, or pentagonal number patterns, Pascal's triangle, and the Fibonacci sequence.

a. Triangular numbers

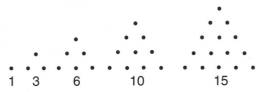

b. Square numbers

c. Pentagonal numbers

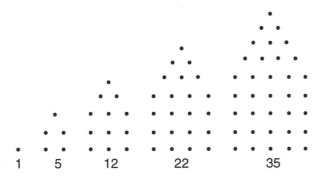

d. Pascal's triangle

```
              1
           1     1
        1     2     1
     1     3     3     1
  1     4     6     4     1
1     5    10    10     5     1
1   6    15    20    15    6    1
```

e. Fibonacci sequence

1, 1, 2, 3, 5, 8, 13, 21, 34, 55, 89, 144, 233, . . .

The Fibonacci Sequence, Branching Patterns, and Flower Petals

1. Look at a flattened piece of parsley and count the branches. Most of the time you will see numbers from the Fibonacci sequence, although nature is not always mathematically perfect! If you can find a sneezewort (*Arcillea ptarmica*) specimen, you'll find that it is an excellent example of the numbers from the Fibonacci sequence. Count branches, leaves, or flowers in this plant. Find some other plants, draw pictures of them, and record their branching patterns. Identify those plants whose branching patterns seem to follow the Fibonacci sequence.

2. Often, the number of petals on a flower will be a Fibonacci number. Try to find at least two of the flowers in the list below, and count and record the number of petals for each flower. Then find a flower that's not on the list and count its petals. See how many different kinds of flowers you can add to the list.

Type of flower	Number of petals
lilies, irises	3
columbines, buttercups, larkspur, primroses	5
delphiniums	8
ragwort, marigolds	13
some asters, some marigolds	21
various daisies	34, 55, 89

Kepler's Fibonacci Relationships

Below are some interesting Fibonacci sequence relationships that were first noted by German astronomer Johannes Kepler (1571–1630). The variable n represents the number of the sequence term. The first relationship merely defines the sequence. Choose three of the relationships, and show that they are true for at least three different values of n.

a. $F_n = F_{n-1} + F_{n-2}$, where $n \geq 3$

b. $F_1 + F_2 + F_3 + \ldots + F_n = F_{n+2} - 1$, where $n \geq 1$

c. $F_1^2 + F_2^2 + F_3^2 + \ldots + F_n^2 = (F_n)(F_{n+1})$, where $n \geq 1$

d. $F_1 + F_3 + F_5 + \ldots + F_{2n-1} = F_{2n}$ where $n \geq 1$

e. $F_2 + F_4 + F_6 + \ldots + F_{2n} = F_{2n+1} - 1$, where $n \geq 1$

f. $F_n^2 = (F_{n-1})(F_{n+1}) + (-1)^{n-1}$

g. $F_n^2 + F_{n+1}^2 = F_{2n+1}$

ACTIVITY 7

Fibonacci Counts Pathways

For each figure, find the total number of ways to get from point A to point B. Describe your results.

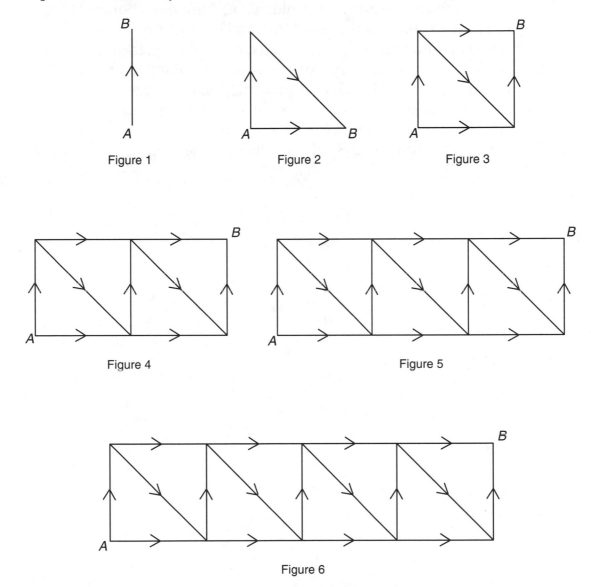

Figure 1 Figure 2 Figure 3

Figure 4 Figure 5

Figure 6

Fibonacci and Architecture

An interesting relationship between the Fibonacci sequence and
architecture exists in the Modular, a modern system of proportion
used in art and architecture. The Golden Ratio and the Fibonacci
sequence are the basis of these architectural proportions
developed in this century by the French architect, painter, and
sculptor Le Corbusier. Do some research on the Golden Ratio and
its relationship to the Fibonacci sequence. Then investigate the
relationship between the Fibonacci sequence and the Modular.
A good source of information is Jay Kappraff's *Connections*, which
is listed in the Resources and Selected Readings section.

ACTIVITY 9

The Golden Rectangle and the Golden Ratio

In the diagram below, *AEFD* and *BCFE* are both Golden Rectangles. Let the length of line segment *DC* = 1 and the length of line segment *CF* = *x*. Set up a proportion and solve for *x* to find the exact value for the Golden Ratio.

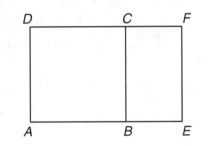

The Golden Rectangle Is Everywhere!

Choose one.

1. Find as many examples as you can of Golden Rectangles in packaged grocery products.

2. Find as many examples as you can of Golden Rectangles in everyday objects you might find at home or at school.

3. Find pictures of flags from different states or countries. See if the overall size of any of the flags is a Golden Rectangle. Can you find any Golden Rectangles in the flag designs?

4. Find examples of Golden Rectangles in architecture. You might want to investigate the Pyramid of Cheops and the Parthenon.

5. Find examples of Golden Rectangles in art. Some artists you might want to investigate are Leonardo da Vinci, Albrecht Dürer, Georges Seurat, Piet Mondrian, Salvador Dali, and George Bellows.

6. Collect several leaves from the same tree or plant, and draw a rectangle around each leaf. Examine the ratio of the length of the rectangle to the width. How often do you find the Golden Ratio, that is, a ratio of the length to the width of approximately 1.61?

ACTIVITY 11

More Golden Ratios

There are many Golden Ratio relationships in the Lute of
Pythagoras, shown here. Measure line segments, and find as
many examples as you can where this ratio exists. (You may
want to label some more points.)

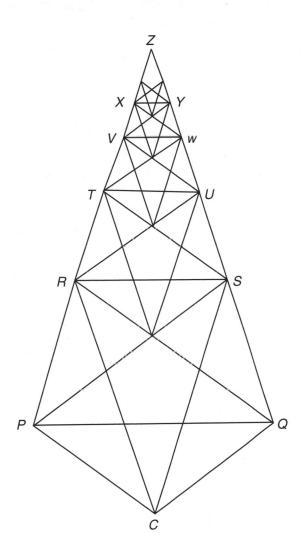

A Ring of Pentagons

One of the wonderful surprises in designing the Lute of Pythagoras quilt was the fact that the pentagons did in fact piece together to form a ring. Trace one of the regular pentagons below. Continue tracing more pentagons until they have formed a ring. How many pentagons do you need to form a complete ring? Use the exterior angle theorem to explain why you can form this ring.

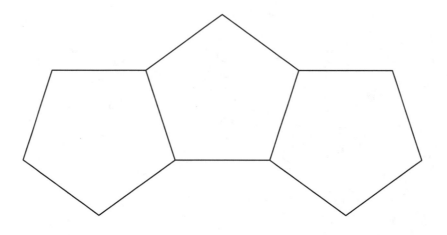

Mathematical Quilts—No Sewing Required!
©1999 Key Curriculum Press

Golden Triangles and Logarithmic Spirals

Triangle *ABC* is a Golden Triangle, and the spiral approximates a logarithmic spiral.

   a. Why do you think this triangle is called a Golden Triangle?

   b. Name as many similar triangles as you can in the figure. (You might need to label some more points.)

   c. Write directions that describe how to construct this spiral if you are given a Golden Triangle.

   d. Trace the Golden Triangle, and try out your construction method.

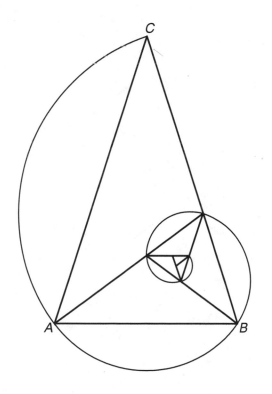

Tying a Pentagon

Get a long strip of paper (adding machine tape works quite well).
Make a loop, pull one of the ends through the loop, and flatten
the knot. If you lift your paper up to the light, you should see a
pentagon. Do you think this figure is a regular pentagon?
Explain why or why not.

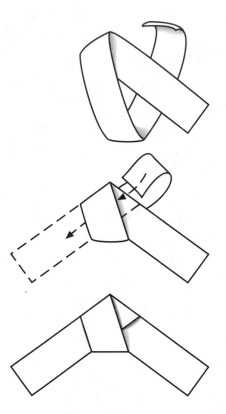

Mathematical Quilts—No Sewing Required!

Pentagons and the Law of Sines

You can often use the Law of Sines to find the measure of unknown angles or sides in a triangle. The Law of Sines states that for any triangle ABC, $\frac{\sin A}{a} = \frac{\sin B}{b} = \frac{\sin C}{c}$. For the pentagon shown here, use the Law of Sines to show that $\frac{CE}{AE} \approx$ Golden Ratio.

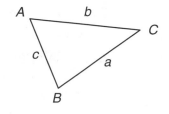

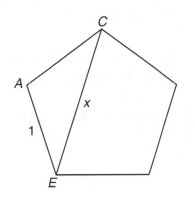

Graphing Calculator Explorations

1. If you have a calculator with a sequence mode, explain how to generate the Fibonacci sequence using this mode.

2. a. Calculate the sequence of numbers generated by the ratios of successive pairs of the Fibonacci sequence:

$$\frac{1}{1} = 1, \frac{2}{1} = 2, \frac{3}{2} = 1.5, \frac{5}{3} = ?, \ldots$$

Explain how your results are related to the Golden Ratio, which is $\frac{1 + \sqrt{5}}{2}$.

b. Enter the lists defined below into your calculator. Then make a scatter plot showing L1 on the horizontal axis and L2 on the vertical axis. Use a window of [0, 13, 1, 0.8, 2.1, 0.1]. Explain what happens in the graph as you continue to divide a lower Fibonacci number into a higher Fibonacci number.

L1—the term number (1, 2, 3, . . . , 12)

L2—the Fibonacci sequence starting with term 1 (1, 1, 2, . . . , 144)

L3—the Fibonacci sequence starting with term 2 (1, 2, 3, . . . , 233)

L4—L3 ÷ L2

3. The proportion used to solve for the Golden Ratio is $\frac{x}{1} = \frac{1}{x + 1}$.

a. Rewrite this proportion as a quadratic equation.

b. Use the quadratic formula and find the exact values for the roots of the equation you found in part a. Use your calculator to evaluate the expression and the approximate values for the roots.

c. Graph the quadratic equation you found in part a. Zoom in on the graph to find the approximate values of the roots.

Mathematical Quilts—No Sewing Required!
©1999 Key Curriculum Press

Graphing Calculator Explorations (continued)

    d. Use the solver on your calculator to find the roots of the quadratic equation you found in part a.

    e. Compare your answers to parts b and c. Which method provides you with the best value for the roots? Which method do you prefer?

    f. What is the relationship between the two roots of the quadratic equation you found in part a?

4. You will probably be surprised to see what happens when you evaluate the continued fraction shown below.

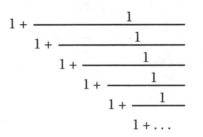

To evaluate this fraction on the HOME screen, follow this procedure:

1 [ENTER]
1 + 1/Ans▶Frac [ENTER] [To access▶Frac, press [MATH] 1.]
Continue pressing [ENTER]

Describe what happens.

5. You can graph polygons and star polygons on your graphing calculator in either polar or parametric mode.

    a. Set your calculator to polar mode. Enter the equation $r = 3(\sin(\theta))$. Set a friendly window and appropriate values for θmin, θmax, and θstep. Experiment by changing these values to create polygons and star polygons. Report on your findings.

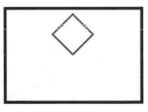

b. Set your calculator to parametric mode. Enter the equations $x = 3\sin(t)$ and $y = 3\cos(t)$. Set a friendly window and appropriate values for Tmin, Tmax, and Tstep. Experiment by changing these values to create polygons and star polygons. Report on your findings.

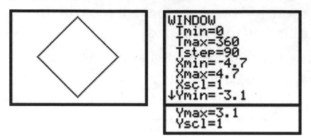

Mathematical Quilts—No Sewing Required!
©1999 Key Curriculum Press

ACTIVITY 17

Internet Explorations

1. An interesting article, "Fibonacci Numbers and the Golden Section," can be found on this Web site:

   http://www.mcs.surrey.ac.uk/Personal/R.Knott/Fibonacci/fib.html.

   Read the article, and write several paragraphs summarizing what you learned.

2. Do an Internet search on Fibonacci, the Golden Rectangle, the Golden Ratio, or the Divine Proportion. Report on your findings.

The Fibonacci × 4 Quilt

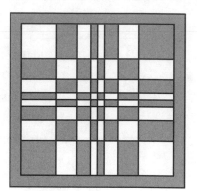

The design for the Fibonacci × 4 quilt explores the Fibonacci sequence in two dimensions. For the quilt shown here, alternate squares were shaded dark to reveal the design of the quilt and to emphasize its symmetry. Notice the squares that emerge on the diagonals.

As with most designs, the addition of shading or color brings the pattern to life and helps you "see" patterns you might not have noticed. The quilt designer chose bold, contrasting colors of bright blue and white for this quilt. An interesting visual aspect of this quilt is its "shimmering" effect. The alternating dark and light colors strike different parts of the retina, causing a visual flashing sensation.

Designing Your Quilt

1. Use grid paper, letting each square represent one unit. Mark off the sequence 1, 1, 2, 3, 5, 8 to the right of the center and then to the left. The 1, 1 sequence should be in the center of the design and thus is part of both the left and right sequences. Draw vertical lines to divide the plane into bars.

    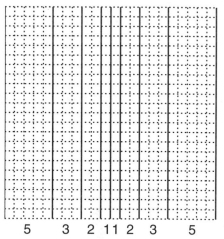

    Repeat the marking-off process on the vertical axis, and draw horizontal lines. At this point, you should have a grid of rectangular boxes with horizontal, vertical, and diagonal symmetry.

2. Look at the quilt design you drew in part 1, and list the dimensions of all the rectangles (including the squares). How many of the rectangles approximate Golden Rectangles?

3. Decide on a color pattern for your quilt, and color your quilt design.

Mathematical Quilts—No Sewing Required!
©1999 Key Curriculum Press

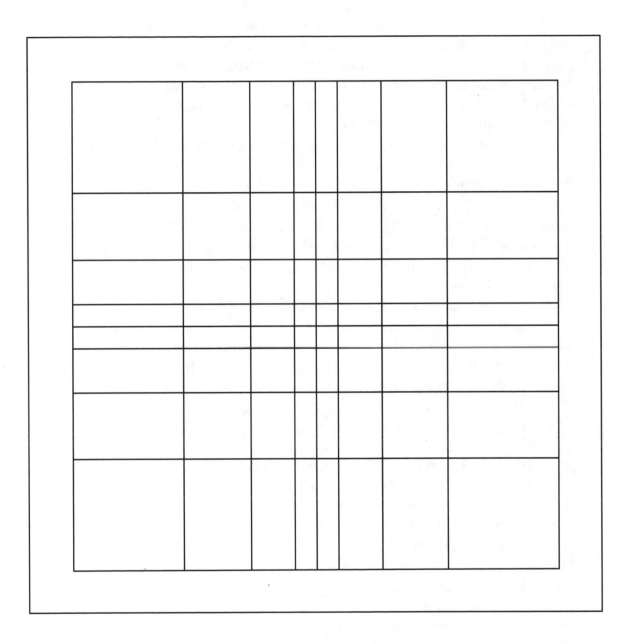

Making the Fibonacci × 4 Quilt

The Fibonacci × 4 quilt requires some planning. Draft the design on large sheets of graph paper, letting the grid spacing represent the construction unit. You might need to tape several sheets of graph paper together to accommodate the complete design. Starting at the center, draw the 1, 1 sequence as four squares. Then draw the remaining rectangular sections in each quadrant. Shade alternate sections with a colored pencil.

Two 100 percent cotton fabric—a bright blue print and a textured white fabric—were selected for the quilt shown on the cover. Two-color quilts are traditional, especially using a bright color along with white as a contrast. For a large 44″ × 44″ quilt made up of four smaller 22-inch squares, you will need 2 yards of each color of fabric. For the small quilt described here, 1 yard of each fabric is sufficient. You will need extra fabric for the borders, backing, and binding.

Because the pattern for the quilt design of the Fibonacci sequence is much like a traditional quilt pattern with rectangular-shaped pieces, you should not have any unusual problems constructing it. In a traditional quilt, the size of each finished square is usually between an 8-inch square and a 12-inch square. The finished size of the complete Fibonacci square is 44″ × 44″, which is difficult to construct as one square. This quilt is much easier to construct if you see it as having four quadrants. Break each quadrant down into its component pieces and list the measurements of each piece. Sew the pieces together to form rows, sew the rows into quadrants and then sew the quadrants together to form the finished quilt.

The table on the following page lists the pieces needed for a small Fibonacci quilt using the sequence 1, 1, 2, 3, 5. Each grid unit used for designing the quilt is translated into a 1-inch unit for sewing the real quilt. Seam allowances of $\frac{1}{4}$ inch were added on each side of each rectangular piece. For the sake of speed and accuracy, you may want to use a rotary cutter to cut the fabric. The finished size for this quilt is 22″ × 22″ without a border. To construct a larger quilt, one which includes more Fibonacci numbers, sketch the quilt design, adding appropriate rectangles to extend the number pattern to 8, 13, and so on.

Fabric for Fibonacci × 4 Quilt

Finished size	Cut size	Number of blue pieces	Number of white pieces	Fibonacci size
1″ × 1″	1.5″ × 1.5″	2	2	1 × 1
1″ × 2″	1.5″ × 2.5″	4	4	1 × 2
1″ × 3″	1.5″ × 3.5″	4	4	1 × 3
1″ × 5″	1.5″ × 5.5″	4	4	1 × 5
2″ × 2″	2.5″ × 2.5″	2	2	2 × 2
2″ × 3″	2.5″ × 3.5″	4	4	2 × 3
2″ × 5″	2.5″ × 5.5″	4	4	2 × 5
3″ × 3″	3.5″ × 3.5″	2	2	3 × 3
3″ × 5″	3.5″ × 5.5″	4	4	3 × 5
5″ × 5″	5.5″ × 5.5″	2	2	5 × 5

Interesting patterns emerge in the table. Because the square pieces on the diagonal belong to both a row and a column, you will need only half as many of these pieces as the nonsquare rectangular pieces. To assemble this design, lay the pieces on a large, flat surface, and assemble them one row at a time, machine-stitching a $\frac{1}{4}$-inch seam. By pressing the seams to alternate sides for each successive row, you will increase the accuracy of the quilt design.

After you have assembled the quilt top, add a border. Layer the quilt top with batting and backing, and baste or pin the three layers together. Machine- or hand-sew along the seam lines. Bind the perimeter of the quilt, and add a rod pocket for hanging.

The Fibonacci × 3 Quilt

The design of this quilt is similar to the Fibonacci × 4 quilt. The difference is that you begin with an equilateral triangle instead of a square. To create the design, you will first need to make a Fibonacci ruler. Once you have your ruler, you can experiment with a variety of polygons to create your own unique quilt design. Notice that the design is slightly off center in this quilt. You may want to experiment by varying the placement of the center in your design.

Designing Your Quilt

1. To construct a Fibonacci ruler, mark divisions of 1, 1, 2, 3, 5, 8 along the edge of a strip of tag board. You might find it helpful to use graph paper to measure the units.

1	1	2	3	5	8

2. Now you can use your Fibonacci ruler to mark the same proportional divisions on a line segment of any length. You will need to recall how to construct a line parallel to a given line through a given point. Study the diagram below, in which all the dashed lines are parallel. Practice dividing several different-length line segments into Fibonacci divisions.

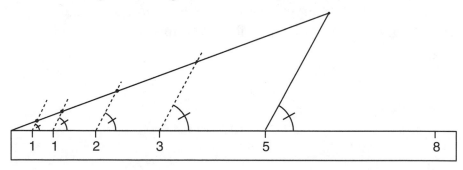

3. Construct an equilateral triangle. Use your Fibonacci ruler and the construction from part 2 to divide each side into Fibonacci divisions. You can center the 1, 1 division, or you can place your design slightly off center. Connect the points on the sides of the triangle to create your design.

Mathematical Quilts—No Sewing Required!
©1999 Key Curriculum Press

Making the Fibonacci × 3 Quilt

The finished Fibonacci × 3 quilt measures 50″ × 42″. For the quilt design shown, you'll need $\frac{1}{4}$ yard each of 11 different fabrics, as well as a different fabric for the background. You will also need a piece of fabric at least 52 inches wide and 44 inches high for the backing. You can piece the backing, or you can use a single piece of fabric, such as an old sheet. You will also need 1 yard of fabric for the quilt border, which is cut on the bias.

The Fibonacci × 3 quilt shown on the cover of this book was sewn using a freezer paper foundation. To use this technique, draw the design of the quilt onto the dull side of the freezer paper. Iron the triangle at the center of the quilt (rose-colored in the quilt on the cover) onto the sticky side of the paper. From there, you can add rows of triangles by first sewing pieced strips together and then sewing the strips onto the center triangle. You can sew the strips in either a clockwise or counterclockwise direction. When using this technique, you may need to do some hand-piecing. Be sure to press each seam as you join the rows.

After you have pieced the triangle together, "float" the triangle on your background. At this point, you can add a decorative border if you want to. An interesting option for a border is to design some blocks based again on the Fibonacci pattern. In general, the fewer triangles in the main body of the quilt, the fancier the border can be.

A flat polyester batting was used for the original quilt. The triangular design was quilted using in-the-ditch stitching. Because of the large amount of negative space in this quilt, the lines of the triangle were extended outward using masking tape. These lines were then quilted using machine stitching. You could experiment with different quilting patterns in the negative space. After binding off the quilt, a tubular sleeve for hanging was added at the top and the bottom of the quilt.

The Fibonacci Sequence and the Golden Rectangle Quilt

The Fibonacci Sequence and the Golden Rectangle quilt contains an artificial spiral that you can easily construct using a compass and straightedge. This spiral only approximates the actual equiangular or logarithmic spiral. The true equiangular spiral cuts the sides of the successive squares at very small angles. This approximation of the spiral touches, or is tangent to, each square.

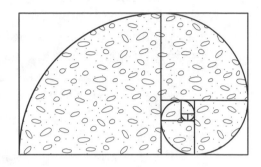

This geometric construction, first demonstrated by German painter and engraver Albrecht Dürer (1471–1528), partitions the Golden Rectangle into smaller, similar, rectangles. That is, each new rectangle is the same shape as the previous rectangle. This phenomenon is called "gnomonic growth," which is a growth pattern associated with living organisms that grow from the inside outwards. (Crystals, on the other hand, grow by agglutination, which is a simple addition of identical elements from the outside, each particle being placed at the most easily reached position.)

Designing Your Quilt

1. Follow these steps to construct a Golden Rectangle with a logarithmic spiral using a compass and straightedge.

   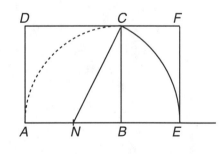

   Step 1 Construct any square $ABCD$.

   Step 2 Find the midpoint of $\overline{AB}$. Call this point N.

   Step 3 Extend $\overline{AB}$. Using $\overline{CN}$ as a radius, draw an arc that intersects $\overline{AB}$ at point E.

   Step 4 Draw a line perpendicular to $\overline{AB}$ at point E.

Step 5 Extend $\overline{DC}$ until it intersects the perpendicular line from point *E*. Label the point of intersection *F*. *AEFD* is a Golden Rectangle.

Step 6 Complete the construction by adding the spiral. Using $\overline{BC}$ as a radius and point *B* as the center, swing arc *AC*. This arc is one-fourth of a circle.

Step 7 Continue nesting Golden Rectangles within the newly formed Golden Rectangle *BEFC*. Construct quarter circles in each square to continue the spiral inwards.

2. You can also create a logarithmic spiral in a Golden Rectangle using paper-folding techniques. Start with a 3- by 5-inch piece of paper, and fold the rectangle using the procedure outlined in part 1. Sketch the quarter circles freehand. Even though this technique is fast and results in a fairly accurate equiangular spiral, you will only be able to do three or four folds.

3. You can also construct a Golden Rectangle with a logarithmic spiral using a sheet of graph paper. Draw a 1×1 square near the lower right-hand side of the paper. Then draw another 1×1 square adjacent to and to the left of the first square. Draw a 2×2 square below and adjacent to the two 1×1 squares. Next, draw a 3×3 square, and place it adjacent to and to the right of the 2×2 and 1×1 squares. Continue drawing squares in a spiraling pattern. To create the logarithmic spiral, use a compass to construct the quarter circles.

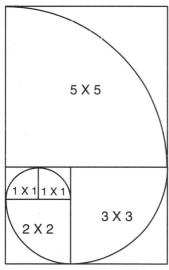

4. Choose one of your Golden Rectangle constructions, and design your quilt. You will need to decide whether to use small squares, as shown in the actual quilt, or large areas of color that emphasize the spiral nature of the design.

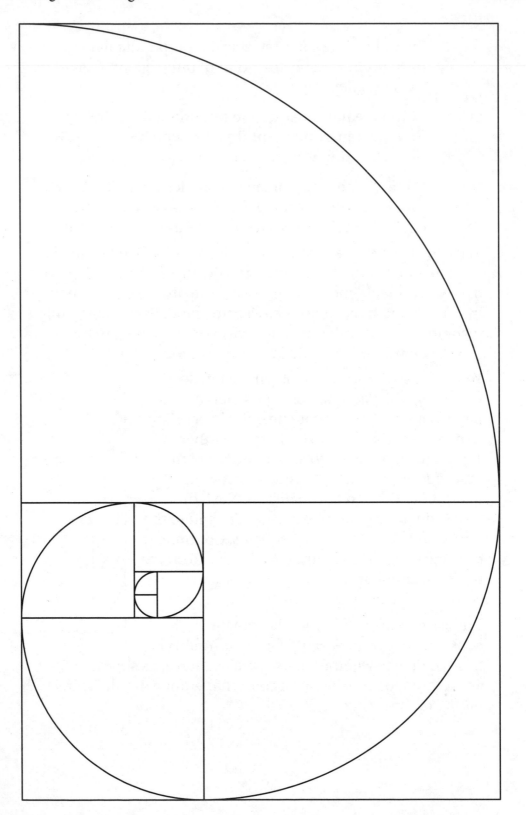

Making the Fibonacci Sequence and Golden Rectangle Quilt

The finished size of the quilt shown on the cover of this book is
43″ × 66″. You will need a 4- by 6-foot piece of fabric for the backing
and 1 yard of fabric for the border, which is cut on the bias. You will
also need $\frac{1}{8}$ yard, or scraps, of 55 different colors of fabric to make the
quilt using the design shown, as well as 1 yard of fabric for the outer
part of the quarter circles to outline the equiangular spiral.

The quilt was pieced with a strip-piecing technique, although a freezer
paper technique would work as well. No matter which technique you
choose, you can make the quilt in various sizes. The quilt shown is
composed of 1-inch squares. By the time you piece the 55-inch square,
the quilt will be quite large. But you could easily stop at the 34-inch or
the 21-inch square and still have an interesting quilt.

Begin piecing at the pole or starting spot of the spiral, which is
located on the two 1-inch squares. In the quilt shown, find the two
1-inch squares that are green and gold, adjacent to each other.
Appliqué a quarter circle onto one of the squares. (Because of the
thickness of the white fabric used in the quilt, it was impossible to
appliqué a quarter circle in the 1-inch square. If you start with a larger
square, this will not be a problem, but the overall size of the quilt will
be affected.) You will probably have to hand-appliqué the smaller
quarter circles. You can machine-appliqué the larger quarter circles.

After sewing the 1-inch squares adjacent to each other, appliqué a
quarter circle on the 2-inch square and sew it below the 1-inch squares.
Next, sew the 3-inch square with its quarter circle appliquéd to the right
of the 1-inch and 2-inch squares.

Then sew the 5-inch square with its quarter circle appliquéd above the
1-inch and 3-inch squares. Now comes the 8-inch square with its quarter
circle appliquéd, positioned to the left of the 5-inch, 1-inch, and 2-inch
squares. Continue spiraling squares until your quilt is the desired size.

When the top of the quilt is completely pieced, insert a fairly flat
batting between the top layer and the backing. A cotton batting was
used for the quilt shown on the cover. Machine-quilt by stitching in-
the-ditch every five squares. To add emphasis to the spiral, quilt the
edge of the spiral as well. After binding the quilt, add a tubular sleeve
at the top and bottom of the quilt for hanging.

The Lute of Pythagoras Quilt

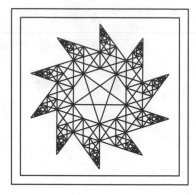

The Lute of Pythagoras appeared on the cover of *The Mathematics Teacher* in February 1989. Rochelle Newman designed a colorful and exciting cover that had beautiful mathematics hidden within. Star patterns, such as the lute, are similar to designs used by Native Americans in clothing and in quilts as imitations of nature and as a sign of power or protection from evil spirits. According to folklore, green stood for grass or trees, red for the sunset, blue for the sky, and yellow for the dawn. The colors in the Lute of Pythagoras quilt represent the colors of winter or a snowstorm. This quilt was pieced during the great Indiana ice storm of 1991, when ice and snow dominated the landscape. Five days without power encourages artists to be creative!

The basic unit of construction for the Lute of Pythagoras quilt is the pentagon. The Pythagorean pentagram (a five-pointed star) was the mystic symbol of the ancient Greek Pythagorean brotherhood and the diagram with which Goethe's Faust trapped Mephistopheles. According to H. E. Huntley:

> The Pythagoreans, who were interested in such matters, regarded the dodecahedron as being worthy of special respect. By extending the sides of one of its pentagonal faces to form a star, they arrived at the pentagram, or triple triangle, which they used as a symbol and badge of the Society of Pythagoras. By this sign they recognized a fellow member.

Nature's pentagrams have been studied throughout the ages. Some examples of pentagons in nature include flowers, starfish, sand dollars, DNA molecules, apples, and leaflets of tomatoes.

The construction of the Fibonacci Sequence and the Golden Rectangle quilt continues inward until you can no longer create more rectangles because they become too small. The construction of the Lute of Pythagoras quilt extends outwards, but the pentagons become smaller and smaller, so again you are limited by the decreasing size. As this construction proceeds outwards, every line segment is in the Golden Ratio to the next-smaller one. The Lute of Pythagoras contains many Golden Triangles. While you are designing this quilt, you will learn how to construct a Golden Triangle.

Designing Your Quilt

1. To construct the design for the Lute of Pythagoras quilt, you will first need to construct a Golden Rectangle. Then you will construct a Golden Triangle and a pentagon, followed by a laddering of pentagons constructed on the base of each isosceles triangle.

   Step 1   Construct a Golden Rectangle. Make your construction marks lightly, because you will want to erase some of them before continuing with step 3.

   a. Construct any square *ABCD*.
   b. Construct the midpoint of $\overline{AB}$. Call this point *N*.
   c. Extend $\overline{AB}$. Using $\overline{CN}$ as a radius, draw an arc that intersects line *AB* at point *E*.
   d. Construct a line perpendicular to line *AB* at point *E*.
   e. Extend $\overline{DC}$ until it intersects the perpendicular line from point *E*. Label the point of intersection *F*. *AEFD* is a Golden Rectangle.

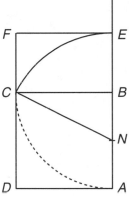

   Step 2   Erase your construction marks and some of the labels so that your Golden Rectangle looks like the one shown here.

Step 3 Using $\overline{AE}$ as the radius and point A as the center, make an arc inside the rectangle. Make another arc using the same radius with the center at point D. Label the intersection of the two arcs as point Z. Triangle DZA is a Golden Triangle.

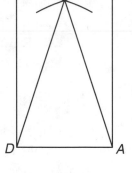

Step 4 Draw an arc with a radius of AD centered at A. Label its intersection with $\overline{DZ}$ as point S. Draw another arc with the same radius centered at point D. Label its intersection with $\overline{AZ}$ as point R. Connect S to R to form $\overline{SR}$, the side length of the pentagon.

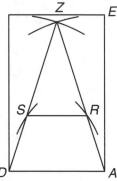

Step 5 Draw an arc with $\overline{SR}$ as the radius and point D as the center. Draw another arc with the same radius centered at point A. Label the intersection as point C. $ACDSR$ is a regular pentagon.

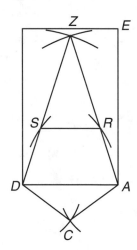

Mathematical Quilts—No Sewing Required!
©1999 Key Curriculum Press

Step 6 Erase the rectangle and construction arcs. Draw the diagonals of each pentagon to form pentagrams.

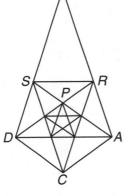

Step 7 Use *SP* as the side length of a new pentagon, and continue the construction upward toward point *Z*.

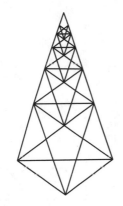

2. Make multiple photocopies of the lute you constructed. Cut them out and arrange them to form a design. You can arrange the lutes in a ring, as was done in this quilt, or you might find another arrangement that you like even better.

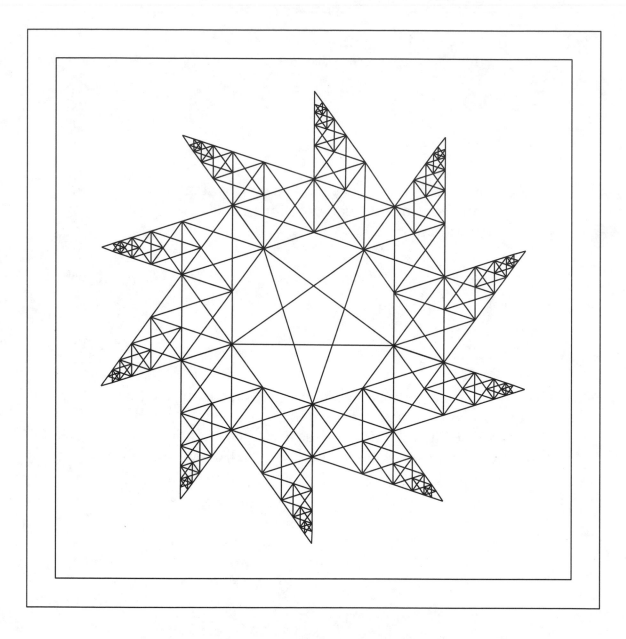

Making the Lute of Pythagoras Quilt

This quilt is 43″ × 43″ inches, so the backing needs to be at least this large. The border requires $\frac{3}{4}$ yard of fabric, which should be cut on the bias. To create the quilt shown on the cover, white and gold lamé threads were used for the quilting, 14 light colors for the lutes, and gold lamé material in portions of the lutes. If you decide to use lamé, use a fray check substance, which can be found in the fabric store. When pressing the pieced items, carefully press over the lamé.

To begin the quilt design, make a large plastic template for the lutes. Using a template will ensure that each lute is the same size when completed.

After designing the quilt on paper, assemble each of the 10 lutes. Although neither paper piecing nor a paper foundation was used when making this quilt, you might find either of these techniques helpful in containing the stresses and strains of the various fabric directions.

When the 10 lutes are complete, "float" them on a plain background fabric. You could appliqué the lutes onto the background. This quilt, however, was not constructed this way. Each individual lute was paired with a gusset piece and joined to the next lute. If you decide to "float" the lutes, you will not need to add the inside decagon. Otherwise, you have to add the decagon by hand at the end.

The quilting of the piece, after the batting was inserted, was a treat! Use half-inch masking tape to "draw" the lines you want to quilt. In this particular quilt, the parallel lines uncovered stars, Golden Triangles, trapezoids, rhombuses, parallelograms, and more. The negative spaces of this quilt are exciting and surprising.

TEACHER NOTES

The connections that mathematicians have discovered among the Fibonacci sequence, Pascal's triangle, and the Golden Ratio are interesting for students to explore. Why these connections occur is not as important for students in the middle and high school grades to understand as the fact that they do occur. Not many mathematical discoveries exist in isolation. Often, they are connected to other topics in mathematics, science, and other real-world situations.

It would be helpful for students to have access to biology or botany books for activities that ask them to explore the Fibonacci numbers related to branching patterns of plants and petal patterns in flowers. Encourage students to search for examples in books or on the Internet.

In Activities 1–8, students explore the Fibonacci sequence. In Activity 1, they make connections between the Fibonacci sequence and Pascal's triangle. In Activities 2–4, they investigate patterns that exist among polygonal numbers, the Fibonacci sequence, and Pascal's triangle. In Activity 5, they explore some connections between the Fibonacci sequence and plant growth. Then in Activity 6, they investigate some number theory relationships that Kepler discovered with the Fibonacci sequence. In Activity 7, they explore another counting relationship that exists between the Fibonacci sequence and pathway patterns. And in Activity 8, they research the relationship between the Fibonacci sequence and architecture.

In Activities 9 and 10, students explore Golden Rectangles and Golden Ratios. Activities 11 and 12 provide an introduction to relationships that exist between pentagons and decagons and that form the basis of the design for the Lute of Pythagoras. In Activity 13, they investigate the Golden Triangle and are introduced to the concept of a logarithmic spiral. In Activity 14, they "tie" a pentagon out of adding machine tape. In Activity 15, they are introduced to the Law of Sines and use the law to discover a Golden Ratio relationship in the regular pentagon.

The Spiraling Squares quilt has some interesting connections to the Fibonacci sequence and the Golden Ratio. The introduction to the Spiral Quilts section develops this connection. Activity 4 in The Right Triangle Quilts section explores an interesting relationship between right triangle triples and the Fibonacci sequence.

The first quilt in this section, the Fibonacci × 4, is based on a design created in a square using a two-dimensional representation of the Fibonacci sequence. The second quilt, the Fibonacci × 3, extends this idea to an equilateral triangle and other polygons. The third quilt, the Fibonacci Sequence and the Golden Rectangle, introduces students to an approximation of the logarithmic spiral created in a series of squares that form a Golden Rectangle. The fourth quilt, the Lute of Pythagoras, is based on a construction that contains regular pentagons, Golden Triangles, pentagrams, and a decagon. Students will create the designs using graph paper, paper folding techniques, and compasses and straightedges. If your students have access to dynamic geometry software such as *The Geometer's Sketchpad,* they can create their quilt designs on a computer.

Answers and Comments

Activity 1

In the first month, there is one pair of rabbits. In the second month, there is still one pair of rabbits because they are not old enough to reproduce. At the beginning of the third month, you have two pairs of rabbits—the original pair and the first pair of offspring. By the fourth month, you have three pairs of rabbits—the original pair and two pairs of their offspring. (The first pair of offspring are not yet old enough to reproduce.) By the fifth month, you have five pairs—the original pair, three pairs of their offspring, and offspring from the first pair of offspring of the original pair. If you continue counting pairs of rabbits each month, you will generate the Fibonacci sequence.

Activity 2

If you sum the numbers on the diagonals in Pascal's triangle, you will get the Fibonacci numbers.

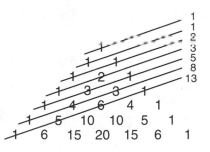

Activity 3

a. The first eight triangular number are 1, 3, 6, 10, 15, 21, 28, 36.

b. The first eight square numbers are 1, 4, 9, 16, 25, 36, 49, 64.

c. The first eight pentagonal numbers are 1, 5, 12, 22, 35, 51, 70, 92, 117.

Activity 4

Answers will vary. See the answer to Activity 2. You can find the triangular numbers in the third diagonal row in Pascal's triangle. You can find the square numbers by adding pairs of triangular numbers. You can find the pentagonal numbers by adding a square number and the previous triangular number.

	1	3	6	10	15 + . . . (triangular numbers)
	1	4	9	16	25 + . . . (square numbers)
		+ 1	+ 3	+ 6	+ 10 + . . . (add the triangular numbers)
	1	5	12	22	35

Activity 5

Answers will vary.

Activity 6

Answers will vary. You can ask students in an advanced mathematics class to prove these relationships using induction.

Activity 7

For Figure 1, there is one pathway; for Figure 2, there are two pathways; for Figure 3, there are 3 different pathways; and so on. The figure shown here summarizes the relationship between the figures and the Fibonacci sequence.

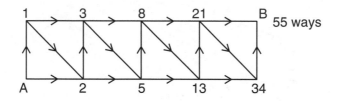

Activity 8

Answers will vary. If any students do a research project on this subject, you might ask them to make presentations to the class.

Activity 9

$$\frac{1+x}{1} = \frac{1}{x}$$
$$x^2 + x - 1 = 0$$
$$x = \frac{-1 + \sqrt{5}}{2}$$
$$x \approx 0.6180 \text{ or } -1.6180$$
$$\therefore 1 + x \approx 1.6180 \approx \Phi$$

Activity 10

Answers will vary.

Activity 11

Answers will vary.

Activity 12

It takes 10 pentagons to form a ring. The decagon formed from the ring of pentagons would have an exterior angle of $\frac{360°}{10}$ or 36°. Because we know that in a regular pentagon, the angle between the side and one of the diagonals is 36°, we could piece the pentagons adjacent to one another without any space left over.

Activity 13

a. Triangle *ABC* is called a Golden Triangle because the ratio $\frac{AC}{AB}$ is the Golden Ratio.

b. Answers may vary.

c. To construct the logarithmic spiral in the Golden Triangle, first bisect the base angle *A* to get segment *AD*. Now triangle *ABC* is similar to triangle *BDA*. Continue bisecting each lower left angle of each resulting similar triangle. After a number of similar triangles are generated, draw an arc for each 36°-36°-108° triangle using the vertex of the isosceles triangle as the center and the length of the congruent legs as the radius. As with the Golden Rectangle, the resulting spiral will be a logarithmic spiral.

Activity 14

Answers will vary.

Activity 15

Because $AE = 1$ and $CE = x$, the Law of Sines gives the relationship $\frac{\sin 72°}{x} = \frac{\sin 36°}{1}$. Solving for x, you get $\frac{0.9510565}{x} = \frac{0.5877853}{1}$. Therefore, $x = 1.6180338$, and the Golden Ratio is approximately 1.618034.

Activity 16

1. In sequence mode on the TI-82 or TI-83, enter $u(n) = v(n-1)$, $v(n) = u(n-1) + v(n-1)$. Set UnStart $= 1$, VnStart $= 1$, and nStart $= 1$. You can also generate the Fibonacci sequence on the home screen using this routine:

   {1,1} [ENTER]

   {ANS(2), ANS (1) + ANS(2)} [ENTER]

2. a. $\frac{1}{1} = 1; \frac{2}{1} = 2; \frac{3}{2} = 1.5; \frac{5}{3} = 1.\bar{6}; \frac{8}{5} = 1.6; \frac{13}{8} = 1.625;$ and so on. The sequence of ratios approaches the Golden Ratio, $\frac{1 + \sqrt{5}}{2} \approx 1.618$.

   b.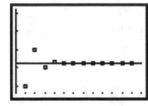

   [0, 13, 1, 0.8, 3.1, .5]

   If you were to draw a horizontal line representing $y = 1.61$, the points would alternate above and below this line, getting closer and closer to it as the term number increases.

3. a. $x^2 - x - 1 = 0$

   b. $\frac{1 \pm \sqrt{5}}{2}$. The approximate values of the roots are 1.618033989 and -0.6180339887.

c. The screens below show the roots found by tracing in a friendly window.

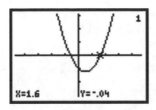 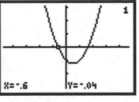 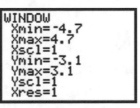

Students could zoom in on the graph to find a more exact value for *x,* or they could zoom in on a table.

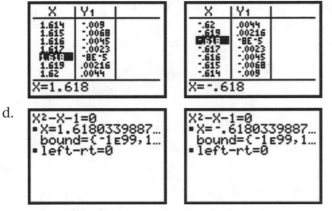

d.

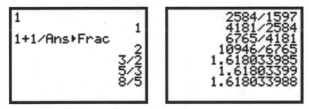

e. Answers will vary.

f. The two roots are reciprocals of each other.

4. These commands generate the Fibonacci sequence, and repeatedly pressing ENTER causes the fractions to eventually become a decimal approximation to the Golden Ratio.

(This activity was adapted from one in the spring issue of *Eightysomething!* entitled "Continued Fractions on Graphing Calculators," by John F. Mahoney.)

5. Answers will vary.

Activity 17

Answers will vary.

TEACHER NOTES

Resources and Selected Readings

Boles, Martha, and Rochelle Newman. *Universal Patterns,* Books 1 and 2. Bradford, MA: Pythagorean Press, 1990, 1992.

Cooke, Theodore A. *The Curves of Life*. New York: Dover, 1979.

Gardner, Martin. *Penrose Tiles to Trapdoor Ciphers*. New York: Freeman, 1989.

Ghyka, Matila. *The Geometry of Art and Life*. New York: Penguin Books, 1987.

Huntley, H. E. *The Divine Proportion*. New York: Dover, 1970.

Jacobs, Harold E. *Mathematics—A Human Endeavor,* 3d ed. New York: Freeman, 1994.

Kappraff, Jay. *Connections: The Geometric Bridge Between Art and Science*. New York: McGraw-Hill, 1991.

Mahoney, John F. *Eightysomething!* The Newsletter for Users of TI Graphing Calculators, Vol. 6, No. 3, Spring 1997.

Pappas, Theoni. *Mathematics Appreciation*. San Carlos, CA: Wide World Publishing/Tetra, 1986.

Pedoe, Dan. *Geometry and the Visual Arts*. New York: Dover, 1976.

Stevens, Peter S. *Patterns in Nature*. Boston: Little, Brown, 1974.

Yates, Robert C. *A Handbook on Curves and Their Properties*. Ann Arbor, MI: Edwards, 1947.

The Spiral Quilts

SPIRALS ARE INTRIGUING SHAPES. HAVE YOU EVER noticed that in some spirals, the loops are spaced at equal intervals, while in other spirals, the intervals between the loops are constantly increasing? If you designed a Golden Rectangle quilt, then you are already familiar with the logarithmic spiral. In this group of quilts, you will investigate several different types of spirals.

Basically, a spiral is a curve traced by a point that moves around a fixed point, from which it moves farther and farther away. The spiral is one of the basic patterns that helps to illustrate the shape of our space. You can find many examples of spiral patterns in nature—in DNA molecules, flower heads, the horns and tusks of animals, some webs, the internal parts of the ear that sense sound, and galaxies and nebulas.

The Wheel of Theodorus Quilt

The Spiraling Squares Quilt

The Indiana Puzzle Quilt

There are two basic spiral shapes that you are likely to encounter in your mathematics and science classes—the Archimedean spiral and the logarithmic spiral. You can generate both spirals using paper-and-pencil techniques.

The Archimedean spiral was named after the great Greek mathematician Archimedes, who wrote a book on spirals. An Archimedean spiral is one in which the loops are spaced at equal intervals so that the distances to the spiral loops form an arithmetic sequence. The sound track on a compact disc is in this shape.

In the logarithmic, or equiangular, spiral, distances from the loops to the center of the spiral form a geometric sequence. As the loops wind outward from the center of the spiral, the spaces become farther and farther apart. More specifically, the spiral is a locus of points that move in a plane so that the tangent at any point forms a fixed angle with the outward-drawn radius vector. The logarithmic spiral was first studied by French philosopher and mathematician René Descartes in 1638. The Italian mathematician Evangelista Torricelli (1608–1647) worked on it independently, and toward the end of the seventeenth century, Swiss mathematician Jakob Bernoulli (1654–1705) discovered many of its remarkable properties. He was so impressed by these almost mystic properties that he had his tombstone engraved with "Eadem mutata resurgo" (Though changed I rise unchanged).

A particularly interesting logarithmic spiral is found in the chambered nautilus, a sea creature that lives in the South Pacific. As it grows, the nautilus shell generates a curve that resembles this spiral. A "gnomonic" growth pattern, such as exhibited by the chambered nautilus, is one in which a shape remains similar to its original form as its size increases. This growth pattern always approximates a logarithmic spiral as a directing curve. In the nautilus shell, each chamber is 6.3 percent larger than the one before. The equiangular spiral is the only type of spiral that does not alter its shape as it grows.

The spiral in the Wheel of Theodorus quilt resembles a nautilus shell. The spiral was first explored by mathematicians searching for the meaning of irrational numbers $\left(\sqrt{2}, \sqrt{3}, \sqrt{5}, \text{ and so on}\right)$. The Greek mathematician Theodorus (circa 400 B.C.) is known for his association with the study of irrational numbers and for his use of the root spiral to explain these numbers. Theodorus belonged to the mathematical group the Pythagorean Society at a time in history when mathematics and astronomy were closely tied to religious beliefs. These mathematicians believed that all numbers could be expressed using whole numbers or the ratio of whole numbers—for example, $0.5 = \frac{1}{2}$, $0.333 = \frac{1}{3}$, and so on. Numbers that can be expressed as the ratio of two whole integers are called rational numbers.

At this time, the Pythagoreans were also exploring square roots, because the Pythagorean theorem for right triangles required the use of square roots. The discovery of the square root of 2, the measure of the hypotenuse of an isosceles right triangle whose legs are each 1 unit in length, caused alarm among the Pythagoreans. (Although the Babylonians had approximated the square root of 2 as 1.414212963 as early as 1700 B.C., Pythagoras is generally credited with the formula we use to determine the lengths of the sides of right triangles.) The Pythagoreans could not find a rational expression that approximated the distance of the square root of 2. How could a number that could not be determined by a ratio of two whole numbers exist in real life as the length of a side of a triangle? More specifically, how could there be a line segment of finite length whose numerical value could not be determined as a ratio? Although you may find it difficult to understand how controversial the discovery of the square root of 2 was, historians realize that understanding irrational numbers helped separate mathematics from religion and helped mathematics become an independent area of study.

There is a connection between spiral growth patterns in flowers and the Fibonacci sequence. Organic forms that grow from the center outward will form a spiral. Upon examination of certain kinds of flowers, one finds seed pockets that spiral left and right. What is curious is that the number of spirals to the left and the number of spirals to the right are different but both are Fibonacci numbers—typically, 55 long spirals and 89 shorter spirals. Some samples have been found with 89 long spirals and 144 short spirals. These successive numbers are called the phyllotaxis number of the plant. For example, the sunflower, with 55 clockwise and 89 counterclockwise spirals, is said to have 55, 89 phyllotaxis. If the spirals in both directions were the same, the pattern of distribution would look like the line drawing of the Spiraling Squares quilt, which has a 1, 1 phyllotaxis.

Pine cone spirals, artichoke spirals, and pineapple spirals also show Fibonacci numbers. If you don't find a Fibonacci number when counting spirals, you might find a Lucas number, named after eighteenth-century mathematician Edouard Lucas. The sequence of Lucas numbers is 1, 3, 4, 7, 11, 18, ... Can you see the relationship between the Fibonacci sequence and the Lucas sequence?

Spiral patterns often appear in the tiny stitches in the handiwork of the Hmong people of Cambodia (see below). The Masai women in Africa often wear spiral-shaped necklaces. These necklaces are used to indicate a woman's age; each year, another brass ring is tied to the necklace, indicating another year in age.

Spiral designs have fascinated mathematicians, scientists, and artists for centuries. In the activities in this section, you will explore the mathematics of various spiral designs and have the opportunity to create your own unique spiral quilt design.

ACTIVITY 1

Exploring the Wheel of Theodorus

In this activity, you will investigate some of the interesting properties of the Wheel of Theodorus.

1. **a.** Find the exact value for the length of each right triangle leg and hypotenuse in the Wheel of Theodorus pictured below (this is not as much work as it might seem). Look for patterns. Create a table like the one shown here, and record your results.

Triangle number	Exact length of the short leg	Exact length of the long leg	Exact length of the hypotenuse	Ratio of successive hypotenuse lengths
1				
2				
3				
. . .				

   b. Find the ratio of the lengths of successive pairs of hypotenuses, and add these results to the table in part a.

   c. Calculate the ratios for the 99th and 100th triangles.

   d. Do the ratios appear to be approaching a limit, that is, a number that the successive ratios are getting closer to but will probably never reach? If so, what is that number?

   e. One of the definitions of a logarithmic spiral is that the ratios of successive radii are always constant. Based on your answers to parts a–d, does the Wheel of Theodorus represent a logarithmic spiral? Why or why not?

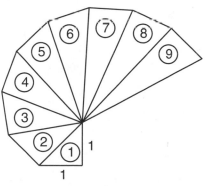

2. Define a trigonometric function that will find the measure of each acute angle at the common vertices of the triangles. Describe what happens to these angle measures as the number of triangles increases.

ACTIVITY 2

Why 17?

Theodorus is cited in Plato's *Theaetetus* as having discussed the irrationality of square roots from 2 through 17 only. Why do you think Theodorus stopped at 17? (*Hint*: Continue adding triangles to the Wheel of Theodorus and see what happens.)

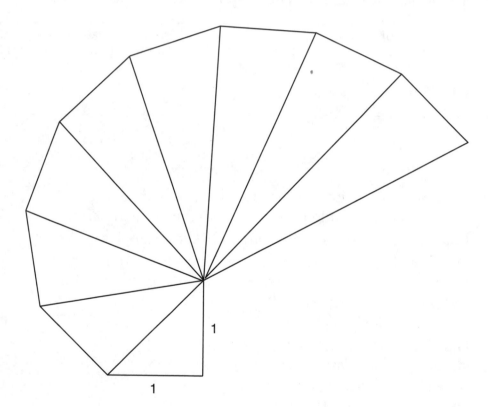

ACTIVITY 3

Side Lengths and Areas of Squares

This pattern begins with the innermost square, with sides whose
length is 1 unit. Use the exact value of the diagonal of this square
as the side length of the next square. Continue computing the
exact value of the side lengths of each successive square.
Complete a table like the one below showing your results.
Describe any patterns you find in the table.

Square	Exact length of each side	Exact length of the diagonal	Area of the square
1	1	$\sqrt{2}$	1
2	$\sqrt{2}$		
3			
. . .			

Rational Number Patterns

With a calculator, you can determine the decimal approximations for irrational numbers very quickly—so quickly, in fact, that sometimes you hardly notice any difference between irrational numbers and rational numbers, especially when you round the results to two or three decimal places. The digits following the decimal point in a rational number will terminate or follow a pattern (for example, $\frac{1}{2} = 0.5$ and $\frac{5}{6} = 0.8333\ldots$). There is no pattern for the digits following the decimal point in an irrational number.

Use a calculator to determine the decimal equivalents in each "family" of rational numbers listed below. Then, on a separate piece of paper, describe the patterns that you discover within and among these sets of decimal equivalents. (*Hint*: Be sure to determine the decimal equivalents for the sevenths to at least eight decimal places. If you're not sure what the pattern is, you may want to do a paper-and-pencil calculation to confirm the pattern.)

$\frac{1}{2} = $ _____ $\frac{1}{3} = $ _____ $\frac{1}{4} = $ _____ $\frac{1}{5} = $ _____

$\frac{2}{3} = $ _____ $\frac{2}{4} = $ _____ $\frac{2}{5} = $ _____

$\frac{3}{4} = $ _____ $\frac{3}{5} = $ _____

$\frac{4}{5} = $ _____

$\frac{1}{6} = $ _____ $\frac{1}{7} = $ _____ $\frac{1}{8} = $ _____ $\frac{1}{9} = $ _____

$\frac{2}{6} = $ _____ $\frac{2}{7} = $ _____ $\frac{2}{8} = $ _____ $\frac{2}{9} = $ _____

$\frac{3}{6} = $ _____ $\frac{3}{7} = $ _____ $\frac{3}{8} = $ _____ $\frac{3}{9} = $ _____

$\frac{4}{6} = $ _____ $\frac{4}{7} = $ _____ $\frac{4}{8} = $ _____ $\frac{4}{9} = $ _____

$\frac{5}{6} = $ _____ $\frac{5}{7} = $ _____ $\frac{5}{8} = $ _____ $\frac{5}{9} = $ _____

$\frac{6}{7} = $ _____ $\frac{6}{8} = $ _____ $\frac{6}{9} = $ _____

$\frac{7}{8} = $ _____ $\frac{7}{9} = $ _____

$\frac{8}{9} = $ _____

ACTIVITY 5

Polygons and Spiraling Squares

Consider the circle diagram below.

a. Use what you know about geometry to find the measures of every angle in the diagram. You shouldn't have to measure any of the angles. Justify your answers. (Because many of the angles have the same measure, you might find it easier to consider one-sixth or one-twelfth of the circle.)

b. How many different squares are there in the diagram?

c. Draw some more lines, and find 12 hidden equilateral triangles.

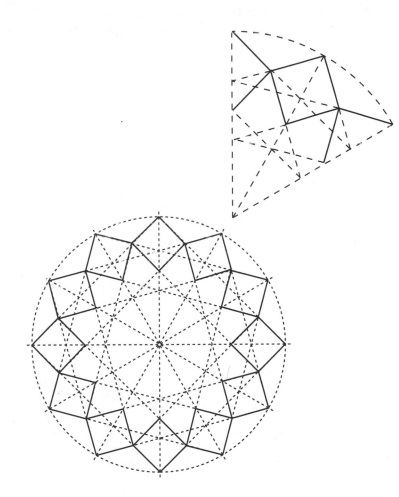

Spiraling Squares
and the Law of Sines

One problem when drawing the spiraling squares design is deciding on an appropriate radius for the starting circle, particularly if you want to start with a certain size square. You can often use the Law of Sines to find the measure of unknown angles or sides in a triangle. The Law of Sines states that for any triangle ABC, $\frac{\sin A}{a} = \frac{\sin B}{b} = \frac{\sin C}{c}$.

Using the Law of Sines, determine a method to find the radius of the starting circle if you want the smallest-size square to have a side length of 1 unit.

Mathematical Quilts—No Sewing Required!
©1999 Key Curriculum Press

Logarithmic Spirals

The Indiana puzzle spirals are logarithmic spirals because the ratios between the successive radii of the spirals remain constant. A radius is a segment from the center of the spiral to the vertex of a triangle. Measure the radii shown in the spiral pictured below, and calculate the successive ratios to show that this spiral is logarithmic.

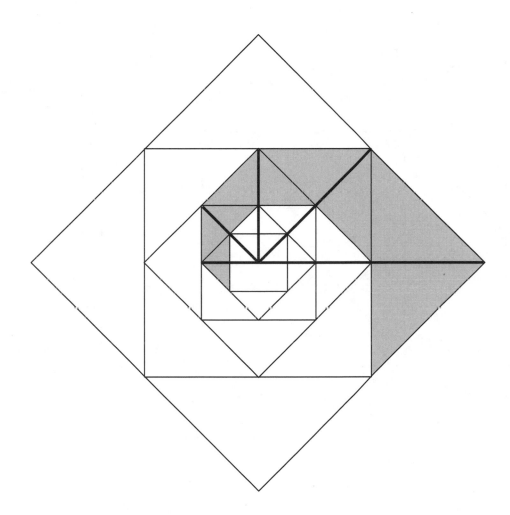

Square Patterns

The design in the Indiana Puzzle quilt results from the square design shown below. While this pattern is identical to Activity 3, now think of it as beginning with the outer square, with the pattern moving inward. Find as many different patterns and relationships as you can in this square pattern.

ACTIVITY 9

Researching Spirals

1. You can use an Archimedean spiral to trisect an angle. Do some research and find out how to do this. Dan Pedoe explains how to do this in his book *Geometry and the Visual Arts*.

2. Read about the connection between spirals and the sacred geometry of the New Jerusalem diagram of ancient cosmology in Jay Kappraff's book *Connections*. Write a short report summarizing your findings.

3. One very interesting relationship is the ideal angle or the Fibonacci angle. As long as a plant stalk is perfectly perpendicular to the ground, the ideal angle is the angle that would allow no two leaves to be exactly over one another (although, of course, maximum exposure is not always desirable for a plant). The ideal angle can be found by multiplying the total number of degrees in a circle, 360°, by the fraction $\frac{1}{\phi}$ (the reciprocal of ϕ). The result is approximately 222.5°. The angle needed to complete the 360° is 137.5°. Thus, 137.5° is the ideal angle! See Jay Kappraff's book *Connections* for a further discussion of irrational numbers and parsing schemes. Summarize your findings.

This diagram represents the top view of a stem growing perpendicular to the ground. Each leaflet is rotated 137.6°.

Spirals All Around Us

Find as many examples as you can of spirals that occur naturally.
If possible, classify each spiral as Archimedean or logarithmic
(equiangular).

Alpha Spirals

Spirals can be generated in many ways. Alpha spirals are created with letters that are assigned numerical and directional moves on graph or dot paper. For example, for the word *spiral,* you can use the numerical assignments below and the alternate horizontal and vertical moves using the directions **Right**, **Down**, **Left**, and **Up**.

1	A	H	O	V
2	B	I	P	W
3	C	J	Q	X
4	D	K	R	Y
5	E	L	S	Z
6	F	M	T	
7	G	N	U	

Follow these steps to create an alpha spiral:

Step 1 Place a large dot in the center of a piece of dot paper.

Step 2 For the letter **S**, draw a line segment 5 spaces to the **Right**, and hold your pencil there.

Step 3 For the **P**, draw a line segment 2 spaces **Down**, and hold your pencil there.

Step 4 For the **I**, draw a line segment 2 spaces **Left**, and hold your pencil here.

Step 5 Continue drawing segments, using the numbers from the table above to determine the number of spaces and always moving in the same sequence—right, down, left, up—until the design closes upon itself or runs off the paper. Not all designs will be the same.

You can keep track of your moves by looking at the sequences that follow. The second line shows how many spaces to move, and the third line shows what direction to move in.

S P I R A L S P I R A L

5 2 2 4 1 5 5 2 2 4 1 5

R D L U R D L U R D L U

a. Create an alpha spiral for your first name. Use the chart on the previous page to determine the number of spaces to move for each letter in your name. You can use any combinations of direction moves—for example, RDLU, RULD, URDL, and so on. Describe your alpha spiral.

b. Make an alpha spiral for your last name. Describe it. Compare it to the design for your first name.

c. For the word *spiral,* which has six letters, and the four directions, 12 line segments are required to finish the design. The least common multiple of 6 and 4 is 12. Can you find a connection among the number of letters in your name, the four movement directions, and the number of line segments required to complete the alpha spiral for your name? If either your first or last name didn't close on a common multiple, explain what happened.

Graphing Calculator Explorations

1. Follow these steps to simulate a spiraling sunflower design on the TI-82 or TI-83.

   Step 1 Select radian, polar, and dot in the MODE menu. Turn the axes off in the FORMAT menu.

   Step 2 In the y= menu, enter the equation $r_1 = A\theta$.

   Step 3 Set an appropriate window. Try starting with a window of θmin $= 200$, θmax $= 1000$, θstep $= 1.61$ (the Golden Ratio), $x$min $= -2500$, $x$max $= 2500$, $y$min $= -1650$, and $y$max $= 1650$.

   Step 4 Store a value for A. Try starting with $A = \frac{1}{2}(\theta\text{step})\pi$.

   Step 5 Press GRAPH.

   You can change the number of spirals by varying the value of θstep. Remember to change the A-value as well. Experiment to generate other patterns. Summarize your findings.

2. With your calculator set in polar mode, you can graph different spiral patterns. The first equation below represents a logarithmic spiral, the second is an Archimedean spiral, and the third is a three-leafed rose. Be sure to graph these equations in a squared-up window.

   a. $r = 1.5e^{\theta\cot(\pi/3)}$

   Be sure your calculator is in radian mode. Start with a decimal (friendly) window, but set Xscl and Yscl to 0. Set θmin $= 0$, θmax $= 4\pi$, and θstep $= 0.2$. Continue zooming out until you are satisfied with the appearance of the graph. Experiment with changing the values of the constants to see their effect on the graph.

b. $r = 0.01\theta$

Set your calculator in degree mode. (You can also graph this equation in radian mode, but you will have to adjust the window values.) Use the following window values: θmin = 0, θmax = 360, θstep = 10, Xmin = −9.4, Xmax = 9.4, Xscl = 0, Ymin = −6.2, Ymax = 6.2, and Yscl = 0. Experiment with changing the values of the constants to see their effect on the graph.

c. $r = 3 \cos (3\theta)$

Set your calculator in degree mode. (You can also graph this equation in radian mode, but you will have to adjust the window values.) Use the following window values: θmin = 0, θmax = 360, θstep = 10, Xmin = −4.7, Xmax = 4.7, Xscl = 0, Ymin = −3.1, Ymax = 3.1, and Yscl = 0. Experiment with changing the values of the constants to see their effect on the graph.

Mathematical Quilts—No Sewing Required!
©1999 Key Curriculum Press

Internet Explorations

1. Go to this Web site to find out how to trisect an angle using an Archimedean spiral:

   http://mathworld.wolfram.com/trisection.html

2. You can find an interesting investigation related to the Spiraling Squares quilt design using *Geometer's Sketchpad* and *Excel* at the following Web site:

   http://jwilson.coe.uga.edu/emt669/Student.Folders/
   Callinan.Michael/Essays/spirals/Spirals.html

3. This Web site focuses on equiangular spirals:

   http://xahlee.org/SpecialPlaneCurves_dir/EquiangularSpiral_dir/
   equiangularSpiral.html

4. This Web site uses logarithmic spirals to simulate some mollusk shells. There are also links to other logarithmic spiral sites.

   http://www.notam02.no/~oyvindha/loga.html

5. If you have JAVA scripts available, you can interact with logarithmic and Archimedean spirals at this Web site. You'll find other interesting history and connections with spirals here as well.

   http://www-groups.dcs.st-andrews.ac.uk/%7Fhistory/Curves/
   Equiangular.html

The Wheel of Theodorus Quilt

The Wheel of Theodorus is a spiral formed by constructing a series of right triangles on the hypotenuses of preceding triangles. The outer edge of the spiral is formed by straight segments, but its path may be smoothed into a curve. Thus, the path on the outer edges traces a spiral. (In mathematics, many curves are formed by a series of straight lines.)

In the Wheel of Theodorus quilt, which is constructed from 36 right triangles, most of the triangle constructions past the $\sqrt{17}$ triangle place the new triangle under the beginning triangles, with the last hypotenuse equal to $\sqrt{37}$. All of the triangles share a common vertex.

Because of the similarity of the design to a seashell, the quilt designer selected a sand/gold print fabric for alternate triangles. A colorful square-checked fabric was chosen for the remaining triangles, cut so that the right angle corner always coincided with the same colored square in the print. This was intended to be a visual reminder of the right angles, because the changing orientation of the triangles often visually distorts their shape. The finished spiral measured 30 inches wide and 26 inches high.

Designing Your Quilt

1. Follow these steps to construct a Wheel of Theodorus spiral using a compass and straightedge. You will need to remember how to construct a line perpendicular to a given line through a given point to complete the steps here.

   Step 1 Decide on a unit length for the two legs of the beginning isosceles triangle.

   Step 2 Construct a right angle, and use the length you chose in step 1 to mark equal lengths on each side of the angle.

Step 3 Connect the endpoints of the sides to form an isosceles right triangle.

Step 4 Construct a line perpendicular to the hypotenuse of the first triangle at point *A*, and mark the length you chose in step 1 on this segment.

Step 5 Draw the hypotenuse of the new triangle.

Step 6 Continue constructing perpendicular segments at each vertex until your design is complete. When you get to the sixteenth triangle, the triangles will overlap. Draw the remaining radii lightly with pencil so that you can erase them later.

2. This construction method is somewhat easier than the method presented in part 1. Follow these steps to construct a square root spiral using the corner of an index card to form the right angles in the triangles and to mark the lengths of the outside edges of the spiral.

Step 1 Choose one of the corners of the index card, and mark equal lengths on the adjacent sides of the corner.

Step 2 Starting in the center of the paper, use the unit markings on the index card to trace the first right angle and to mark the lengths of the adjacent sides of the angle.

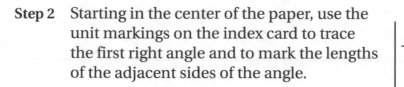

Step 3 Use a straightedge to draw the hypotenuse of the first isosceles right triangle.

Step 4 Place the index card so that one side of the right angle lies on the hypotenuse of the first triangle, with the vertex of the right angle on the index card exactly aligned with the vertex of the hypotenuse and leg of the isosceles right triangle. Trace the segment for the unit leg of the second triangle.

Step 5 Use a straightedge to draw the hypotenuse of the second triangle.

Step 6 Repeat steps 4 and 5, drawing as many triangles as you have room for on the paper. When you get to the sixteenth triangle, the triangles will overlap. Draw the remaining radii lightly with pencil so that you can erase them later.

Mathematical Quilts—No Sewing Required!
©1999 Key Curriculum Press

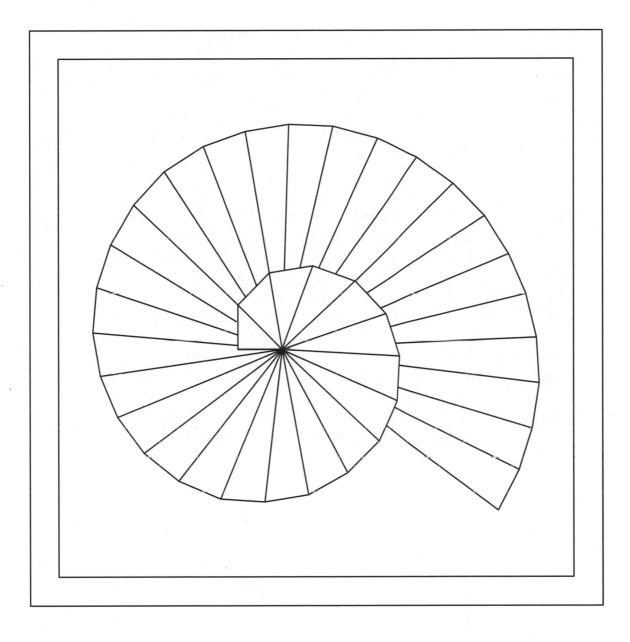

Making the Wheel of Theodorus Quilt

Creating quilts from mathematical designs often requires that you solve some problems and identify the best materials. Some considerations when designing a Wheel of Theodorus quilt are the desired finished size of the design and color selection. An isosceles right triangle with legs measuring 3 inches results in a spiral approximately 30 inches wide, a suitable size for a wall hanging. To make a quilt this size, you will need $\frac{1}{2}$ yard of each fabric used for the spiral, 1 yard of fabric for the background, and $\frac{1}{4}$ yard of fabric for the border.

Cut the 36 triangles from $\frac{1}{4}$-inch wax-coated graph paper. The grid provides an easy way to measure the sides of the triangles, and you can check these measures with your calculator. Cut out the triangles, and iron them to the wrong side of the fabric. Then cut out the fabric triangles, being sure to add a seam allowance. Sew the triangles together in pairs, and then sew the pairs together into units of 4, 8, and so on, until all 36 units are joined. After you complete the spiral, remove the paper and, using invisible thread, stitch the spiral to the background fabric. Insert batting between the layers, and add a border. The quilting design used for the wall hanging shown on the cover of this book was a simple outline of the spiral and the border of the rectangular backing. The purpose of the quilting is to hold the three layers together, and with a wall hanging, minimal quilting is necessary.

The Spiraling Squares Quilt

Look around you. You never know where you might find the inspiration for a mathematical quilt design. An intercom plate in a wall in the Louvre in Paris, France, provided the inspiration for this quilt.

The ratio of the number of squares in each level of the spiral pattern in this quilt is always 1 to 1. This means that the spiral pattern has a 1, 1 phyllotaxis. For plants, the phyllotaxis relationship determines how much sunlight is available for each level of leaves. The phyllotaxis relationship in this design would not permit much sunlight to reach the leaves below. Each new leaf would be directly above the previous leaf, so the lower leaves would be rather starved for sunlight. Under perfect conditions, which only a mathematician can create and nature rarely does, a plant will obtain maximum exposure to sunlight and minimum overlapping of leaves if each leaf is separated from the previous leaf by an angle of about 137.5°. Each of the squares in this spiral design is offset by $\frac{360°}{12}$ or 30°. Even though such a leaf distribution pattern is less than ideal, the design is still an interesting and appealing pattern of squares.

Designing this quilt can be quite complex when you use a compass and straightedge, as outlined in part 1. Part 2 provides you with an easier method for creating the design.

Designing Your Quilt

1. Follow these steps to construct your spiraling squares design. You will need to remember how to bisect an angle, and you will also need to be very careful and precise to complete the design.

   Step 1 Using a compass, draw a circle.

   Step 2 Divide the circle into 12 congruent arcs. To do this, first use the radius to mark off six equal arcs around the circle. Then bisect each arc.

Step 3   Start at each vertex on the circle, and connect every third point. (You will probably have to do some erasing because you will be drawing many lines.) These lines will form the outer sides of the squares.

Step 4   Start at each vertex on the circle, and connect every four of the inner vertices to form the inside sides of the squares.

Step 5   To construct the second layer of squares, extend each of the 12 diameters of the circle. Use your compass to measure the side length of the new square by measuring the length of the diagonal of the original square. To construct and position the new squares, swing the new side length from each common vertex of pairs of the original squares. Complete the construction of the new squares.

Step 6   Continue adding new squares to the outer edge of the pattern until your design is complete.

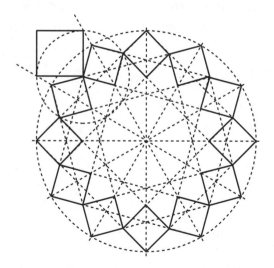

Mathematical Quilts—No Sewing Required!
©1999 Key Curriculum Press

2. Another approach to creating this design is to decide what size squares you want to begin with. Cut a template for this square out of tag board, and determine the needed radius for the beginning circle (refer to Activity 7 as needed to determine the radius). Use a compass to draw the circle. Then divide the circle into 12 equal arcs using either a compass or a protractor, and trace the square into the appropriate positions. Next, make a pattern for the next size square by using the diagonal length of the previous square as the side length for the new square. Continue adding larger and larger squares until your design is complete.

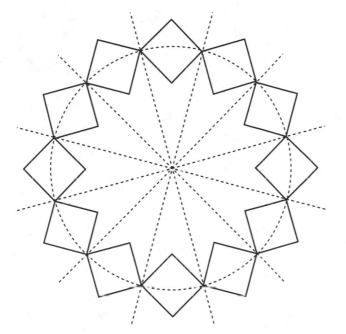

3. Make several photocopies of your spiraling squares design. Cut out the designs and combine them to create a unique mathematical design.

Making the Spiraling Squares Quilt

The completed quilt is 30″ × 30″. You will need 1 yard of fabric for the backing and $\frac{1}{2}$ yard for the border. You will also need 1 yard of fabric for the background and fabric for the appliquéd squares. The thread used to appliqué the quilt should match the fabric of the squares. Gold lamé thread was used in the original quilt to outline each square. For this quilt the squares were cut out of a flowered material and appliquéd onto a navy blue background. You could use a pattern for the background and make the squares out of a plain fabric.

You can make this quilt any size. First, construct the design on the back side of freezer paper. The smallest squares in our quilt were 1 inch by 1 inch. Remember to add $\frac{1}{4}$ inch to each side of each square because the squares will be appliquéd. The key to accuracy in this quilt is establishing the first group of 12 squares in a circular format. Appliqué the new squares between the spaces of the old squares. You might find it helpful to use a fusible interfacing to hold the squares in place while appliquéing them. This is especially true for the small squares in the initial ring.

After you appliqué the top, insert the batting. A gold lamé thread outlining each square helps to make the squares pop out at the viewer and adds a sparkly touch without overpowering the quilt design. If your squares are solid fabric, you can do some creative quilting inside each square.

The quilt shown has a small contrasting border. This border can be pieced or appliquéd after you complete the spiral design. A gold soutache thread was sewn at the junction of the complementary strips.

The Indiana Puzzle Quilt

The pattern in the Indiana Puzzle quilt (also known as the Snail's Trail pattern) is based on one of the spiral patterns called Baravalle spirals. These logarithmic spirals are formed by a nesting pattern of inscribed similar polygons. Quilters historically have been attracted to square designs, which, when combined with copies of themselves, create new visual patterns. The Indiana Puzzle or Snail's Trail is such a pattern. Similar quilt patterns often have different names in different parts of the country as quilters rename patterns to represent their vision of the design illustrated.

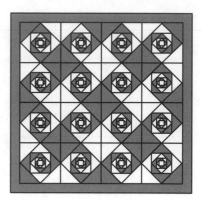

The quilt design for the Indiana Puzzle consists of 16 squares, each of which contains four spirals. When the squares are combined, a far more complex pattern of spirals emerges. This is an example of design synergy, in that the pattern formed by joining 16 squares is far more intricate than its individual components. The Virginia Reel quilt pattern is another pattern that is formed by nesting squares. Its center, however, is a solid square instead of the four-patch center in the Indiana Puzzle quilt.

The recursive pattern of steps that form the spirals in this design resembles the steps used in creating *fractals*—geometric shapes that are formed by repeating steps that result in a characteristic called *self-similarity*. The Indiana Puzzle spiral is formed by repeating the same steps over and over, but the resulting shape is not self-similar. That is, it does not contain many miniature or similar versions of the design within it.

Designing Your Quilt

1. Follow these steps to create the spiral design for the Indiana Puzzle quilt.

   Step 1 Draw a square on graph or square-dot paper. Because you will be bisecting the sides of the square, it's best if the dimensions of the sides are a power of 2.

Mathematical Quilts—No Sewing Required!
©1999 Key Curriculum Press

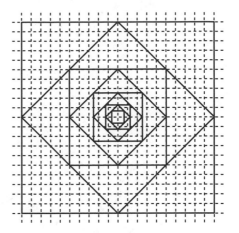

Step 2 Mark the midpoint of each side of the square.

Step 3 Connect the midpoints to form a new square inscribed in the original square.

Step 4 Repeat steps 2 and 3 until you have the desired number of inscribed squares or until the sides of the center square are too short to bisect.

Step 5 To complete the design, shade the similar right isosceles triangles to form a spiral.

2. Follow the steps in part 1, but start by constructing a square with 8 or 16 units per side. Use colored markers or pencils to shade the four spirals in the square.

3. Construct an Indiana Puzzle square on graph or square-dot paper, but do not color or shade the spirals. Make photocopies of the square, and create a color pattern so that the adjoining squares form a synergistic design.

4. You can generate other spiral forms by subdividing the sides of the squares into other ratios. Draw a square whose sides measure a power of 4. Mark a point one-quarter of the measure from the corresponding vertices of each side, and connect these points as in the Indiana Puzzle to form a new square. What is the degree orientation of this square? Continue with this pattern until the center square is too small to subdivide. Shade as for the Indiana Puzzle. Describe the results.

5. Start with a regular hexagon as the original polygon. Use a ruler to find the midpoint of the sides, connect the midpoints, and describe the resulting shape. Repeat this process of marking midpoints and connecting them. Can the resulting design be shaded to form a spiral or spirals? If so, show how the design can be shaded.

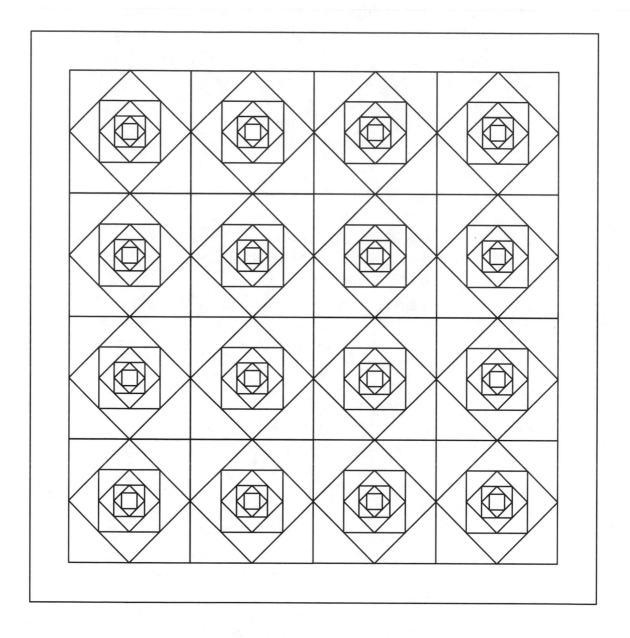

Making the Indiana Puzzle Quilt

The Indiana Puzzle quilt pattern requires a bold contrast in fabric to accent the spiral formations. Traditionally, it is worked in two contrasting colors. The use of a variety of colors in the quilt shown on the cover was an experiment in color design. The quilt designer was interested in the squares formed by the intersection of the four corners of the connecting squares. A multicolored floral print was chosen as the centerpiece for this quilt, and then four other bright complementary-colored fabrics were used for the remaining spirals and a yellow-beige fabric for the background. The pattern for the quilt consists of 16 squares. Each square has one multicolor spiral, one complementary-colored spiral, and two neutral-colored spirals. For this quilt, you will need 1 yard of fabric for the dominant spiral and $\frac{1}{4}$ yard of five different fabrics for the other spirals. You will also need 2 yards of fabric for the background and $\frac{1}{2}$ yard for the border.

Although the pattern for the Indiana Puzzle quilt is a traditional design, modern methods of construction make it easy to sew the fabric pieces together. Because the center pieces of this pattern are very small and difficult to work with, the paper foundation piecing method was used for construction. With this method, 16 pattern squares were photocopied onto paper. Using these paper foundation patterns, the fabric was stitched on the reverse side from the center outward, using the lines on the paper pattern as a stitching guide. (Lesley-Claire Greenberg explains this method in her book *Sewing on the Line—Fast and Easy,* published by That Patchwork Place.) This method of construction requires a new kind of thinking, because the fabric is hidden under the paper during the sewing process. As with most new methods, practice, patience, and persistence are necessary to master the technique.

After the 16 squares were constructed, the squares were stitched together to create the quilt, and a border was added to frame the spiral design. The finished quilt was layered with batting and backing and machine-quilted in a spiral design.

TEACHER NOTES

Students are usually fascinated by spiral designs. These quilts should motivate their interest in the mathematical explorations as well as the design activities.

The visual appeal of the Wheel of Theodorus is usually sufficient encouragement for students to want to reproduce it and explore its relationships. The activities related to this quilt are suitable for students with an elementary understanding of square roots. In Activity 1, students calculate the ratios of successive pairs of hypotenuses. This calculator exercise gives them practice using square roots in an application activity and lets them explore the concept of limit at an elementary level. In the second part of the activity, students use right triangle trigonometric definitions to find the measures of acute angles in the spiral.

In Activity 2, students examine why Theodorus stopped at 17 when computing rational roots. In Activity 3, they explore relationships between side lengths and areas of the squares in the design pattern used to create the Indiana Puzzle quilt.

In Activity 4, students explore rational numbers in "families" to reinforce the concept of repeating and terminating decimals. Often, students work such problems in a textbook assignment but do not get an opportunity to discover the many patterns embedded in rational numbers. Encourage students to explore families of fractions further and to discover relationships among them.

In Activity 5, students look for different polygons in the Spiraling Squares design. In Activity 6, they are introduced to the Law of Sines and use it to find an appropriate radius for a circle to use to start their spiral design. Activity 7, in which students explore logarithmic spirals, does not require an understanding of logarithms. The ratios for the activity are easily measured using units on graph paper. In Activities 8–10, students investigate further some properties of spirals and squares.

In the activities for the Wheel of Theodorus quilt, students can choose between a formal compass-and-straightedge construction or a more informal approach using an index card. No measurements are required with either of these processes. Encourage students to occasionally check the lengths of the sides of the new triangles with a ruler. However, it is not necessary to do any measurements to complete the spiral. At the point where the spiral begins to overlap itself, allow students to solve the problem of how to illustrate the succeeding triangles on paper.

The intriguing pattern in the Spiraling Squares quilt might inspire students to ask if this is the way plants actually grow and spiral. This is an interesting topic to investigate and leads to many possibilities for lesson plans. The activities and the readings offer some options, but many others exist. Let your imagination go!

The symmetry involved in the Spiraling Squares quilt is described as a prime point group rather than a base group symmetry. The growth factor is $\sqrt{2}$. This growth pattern is referred to as a *harmonic growth* between each of the squares in one part of the spiral, because in the next layer the old diagonal is used to determine the length of the side of the next square. The area of each square doubles as each square spirals outward. Students explored this concept in Activity 3.

The construction of the Spiraling Squares quilt design is somewhat difficult. Students can apply what they learned in Activity 6 to simplify this construction. They can work backwards by deciding on the size of the original square and then constructing the appropriate circle and gluing cut-out squares on the design.

The Indiana Puzzle quilt is known by a variety of names. Students may enjoy learning that quilt patterns often have different names in different parts of the country. You might suggest that they name their individual quilt designs. Also encourage them to experiment with shading patterns until they discover the spiral pattern. Have plenty of graph paper available. You could also make copies of Activity 9 for students to use in experimenting with different design possibilities. In Activity 11, they are introduced to alpha spirals, or spirolaterals. You can get more information about spirals by visiting these Web sites:

http://www.astro.virginia.edu/~eww6n/ math/Spirolateral.html

http://www.corona.bell.k12.ca.us/teach/ swa/sam.html

Answers and Comments

Activity 1

1. a.

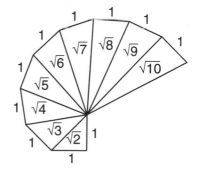

a. and b.

Triangle number	Exact length of the short leg	Exact length of the long leg	Exact length of the hypotenuse	Ratio of successive hypotenuse lengths
1	1	1	$\sqrt{2}$	
2	1	$\sqrt{2}$	$\sqrt{3}$	1.225
3	1	$\sqrt{3}$	$\sqrt{4} = 2$	1.155
4	1	$\sqrt{4} = 2$	$\sqrt{5}$	1.118
5	1	$\sqrt{5}$	$\sqrt{6}$	1.095
6	1	$\sqrt{6}$	$\sqrt{7}$	1.080
7	1	$\sqrt{7}$	$\sqrt{8}$	1.069
8	1	$\sqrt{8}$	$\sqrt{9} = 3$	1.061
9	1	$\sqrt{9} = 3$	$\sqrt{10}$	1.054

c. For the 99th triangle, you would have $\frac{\sqrt{100}}{\sqrt{99}} \approx 1.005038$. For the 100th triangle, you would have $\frac{\sqrt{101}}{\sqrt{100}} \approx 1.004988$.

d. The ratios appear to be approaching 1.

e. The Wheel of Theodorus is not a logarithmic spiral because the ratios of successive radii are not constant even though they appear to be approaching a limit.

2. You could use any of the right triangle trigonometric ratios to find the measure of each angle. The angle measures get smaller as the number of triangles increases.

Activity 2

The seventeenth triangle starts to overlap the previous triangles.

Activity 3

Square	Exact length of each side	Exact length of the diagonal	Area of the square
1	1	$\sqrt{2}$	1
2	$\sqrt{2}$	$\sqrt{4} = 2$	2
3	$\sqrt{4} = 2$	$\sqrt{8}$	4
4	$\sqrt{8}$	$\sqrt{16} = 4$	8
5	$\sqrt{16} = 4$	$\sqrt{32}$	16
6	$\sqrt{32}$	$\sqrt{64} = 8$	32
7	$\sqrt{64} = 8$	$\sqrt{128}$	64
8	$\sqrt{128}$	$\sqrt{256} = 16$	128
9	$\sqrt{256} = 16$	$\sqrt{512}$	256

Activity 4

$\frac{1}{2} = 0.5$

$\frac{1}{3} = 0.\overline{3}$

$\frac{2}{3} = 0.\overline{6}$

$\frac{1}{4} = 0.25$

$\frac{2}{4} = 0.5$

$\frac{3}{4} = 0.75$

$\frac{1}{5} = 0.2$

$\frac{2}{5} = 0.4$

$\frac{3}{5} = 0.6$

$\frac{4}{5} = 0.8$

$\frac{1}{6} = 0.1\overline{6}$

$\frac{2}{6} = 0.\overline{3}$

$\frac{3}{6} = 0.5$

$\frac{4}{6} = 0.\overline{6}$

$\frac{5}{6} = 0.8\overline{3}$

$\frac{1}{7} = 0.\overline{142857}$

$\frac{2}{7} = 0.\overline{285714}$

$\frac{3}{7} = 0.\overline{428571}$

$\frac{4}{7} = 0.\overline{571428}$

$\frac{5}{7} = 0.\overline{714285}$

$\frac{6}{7} = 0.\overline{857142}$

$\frac{1}{8} = 0.125$

$\frac{2}{8} = 0.25$

$\frac{3}{8} = 0.375$

$\frac{4}{8} = 0.5$

$\frac{5}{8} = 0.625$

$\frac{6}{8} = 0.75$

$\frac{7}{8} = 0.875$

$\frac{1}{9} = 0.\overline{1}$

$\frac{2}{9} = 0.\overline{2}$

$\frac{3}{9} = 0.\overline{3}$

$\frac{4}{9} = 0.\overline{4}$

$\frac{5}{9} = 0.\overline{5}$

$\frac{6}{9} = 0.\overline{6}$

$\frac{7}{9} = 0.\overline{7}$

$\frac{8}{9} = 0.\overline{8}$

Here are some patterns that students may notice:

Fractions with denominators of 2, 4, and 8 all terminate because 2 is a prime factor of 10.

Fractions with a denominator of 5 all terminate because 5 is a prime factor of 10.

Fractions with a denominator of 7 have a six-digit repeating pattern. The six digits are always in the same order, but each repeating pattern starts with a different digit.

Fractions with a denominator of 3 or 9 all have a single-digit repeating pattern.

Fractions with a denominator of 6 sometimes repeat and sometimes terminate because $2 \times 3 = 6$.

Family patterns are determined by the prime factors of the denominators.

Activity 5

a.

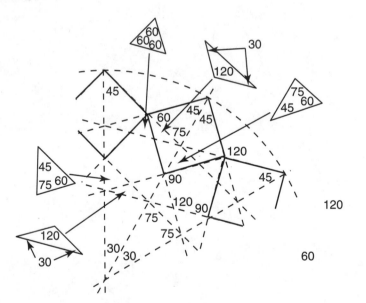

b. 18

c.

Activity 6

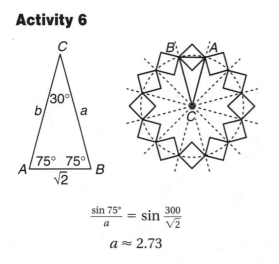

$$\frac{\sin 75°}{a} = \sin \frac{300}{\sqrt{2}}$$

$$a \approx 2.73$$

Activity 7

Student measurements may vary, but the ratios should all be approximately 1.4. Therefore, the spiral is logarithmic.

Activity 8

Answers will vary.

Activity 9

Answers will vary.

Activity 10

Answers will vary.

Activity 11

Answers will vary.

Activity 12

1.

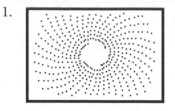

(The calculator routine was provided by Paul Foerster.)

2. a. $r = 1.5e^{\theta\cot(\pi/3)}$ (radian mode)

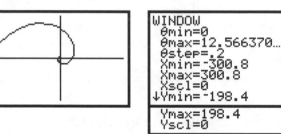

```
WINDOW
 θmin=0
 θmax=12.566370…
 θstep=.2
 Xmin=-300.8
 Xmax=300.8
 Xscl=0
↓Ymin=-198.4

 Ymax=198.4
 Yscl=0
```

  b. $r = 0.01\theta$ (degree mode)

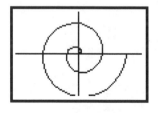

```
WINDOW
 θmin=0
 θmax=720
 θstep=10
 Xmin=-9.4
 Xmax=9.4
 Xscl=0
↓Ymin=-6.2

 Ymax=6.2
 Yscl=0
```

  c. $r = 3\cos(3\theta)$ (degree mode)

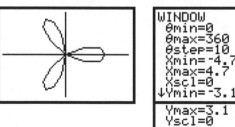

```
WINDOW
 θmin=0
 θmax=360
 θstep=10
 Xmin=-4.7
 Xmax=4.7
 Xscl=0
↓Ymin=-3.1

 Ymax=3.1
 Yscl=0
```

Activity 13

Answers will vary.

Resources and Selected Readings

Boles, Martha, and Rochelle Newman. *Universal Patterns,* Books 1 and 2. Bradford, MA: Pythagorean Press, 1990, 1992.

Davis, Philip J. *Spirals from Theodorus to Chaos.* Wellesley, MA: Peters, 1993.

Kappraff, Jay. *Connections: The Geometric Bridge Between Art and Science.* New York: McGraw-Hill, 1991.

Murphy, Pat, William Neill, and Diane Ackerman. *By Nature's Design.* San Francisco: Chronicle Books, 1993.

Pappas, Theoni. *The Mathematics Calendar.* San Carlos, CA: Wide World Publishing/Tetra, 1993.

Pedoe, Dan. *Geometry and the Visual Arts.* New York: Dover, 1976.

Soltow, Willow Ann. *Quilting the World Over.* Radnor, PA: Chilton Book Company, 1991.

The Right Triangle Quilts

THE DISCOVERY OF THE THEOREM RELATING THE LEGS and the hypotenuse of a right triangle is one of the most profound accomplishments in the history of mathematics. Simply stated, for any right triangle with legs a and b and hypotenuse c, $a^2 + b^2 = c^2$. The converse of the theorem states that if $a^2 + b^2 = c^2$, then the triangle is a right triangle. You can also use this theorem with other polygons because any polygon can be divided into a series of right triangles.

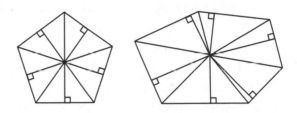

The Greek mathematician Pythagoras (572–497 B.C.) generally is credited with the discovery of the theorem. However, some evidence suggests that the Chinese used a version of this formula in calculating

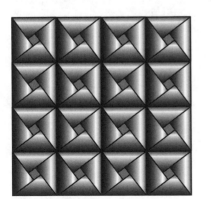

The Behold! Quilt

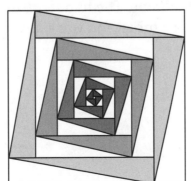

The Pythagorean Triples Quilt

The Spiraling Pythagorean Triples Quilt

measures for right triangles before Pythagoras, and Egyptian mathematicians may have used this right triangle relationship when building the pyramids.

Over 300 proofs of the theorem exist today, some of which are merely simple geometric pictures. One of the simplest, shown here, is sometimes attributed to Pythagoras. The first quilt in this section is based on another pictorial proof attributed to the Hindu mathematician Bhāskara (1114–1185).

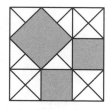

The sets of three integers that represent the lengths of the sides of a right triangle are often called Pythagorean triples. Throughout history, mathematicians have searched for ways to generate these sets of triples, looking for patterns both that exist within the triples and that connect the right triangle triples to other sets of numbers. The best-known set of triples is 3-4-5. All multiples of this set of numbers also satisfy the right angle formula. Other sets of triples, such as 5-12-13 and 7-24-25, are commonly found in mathematics textbooks. In Activities 2 and 3, you will explore sets of right angle triples.

Even though the lives of Pythagoras and Fibonacci were separated by 1700 years, scholars have discovered some interesting relationships between their works. The Fibonacci sequence (1, 1, 2, 3, 5, 8, . . .) is a series of numbers often associated with birth patterns of animals and with plant branching and petal patterns in botany. For any four consecutive Fibonacci numbers—for example, 1, 2, 3, 5—the product of the outer terms ($1 \times 5 = 5$) and two times the product of the inner terms [$2 \times (2 \times 3) = 12$] are numbers that can represent the lengths of the legs of a right triangle. The hypotenuse of this triangle is 13, which is also a Fibonacci number. You will explore this relationship further in Activity 4.

Bhāskara's Proof

According to legend, the Hindu mathematician Bhāskara (1114–1185) drew this square and presented it to his peers with the simple statement, "Behold!" Supposedly, he believed this construction presented a beautiful and obvious proof of the Pythagorean theorem. Use algebra to show why this is indeed proof of the relationship $a^2 + b^2 = c^2$.

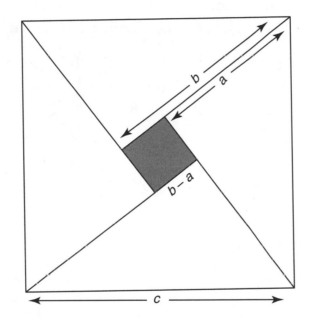

Right Triangles and Squares

The 3-4-5 right triangle was used to create the Behold! quilt design. Can right triangles based on other triples also generate a square? Begin with the 5-12-13 triangle. Draw four of these triangles on graph paper, and cut them out. Can you position the four triangles the same way as the 3-4-5 triangles were to create a square? If so, what are the dimensions of this square? What is the shape in the center?

Repeat this process with the 7-24-25 triangle. Choose any other right triangle triple, and see if you can form a square. Will this process work with any right triangle triple? Explain why or why not.

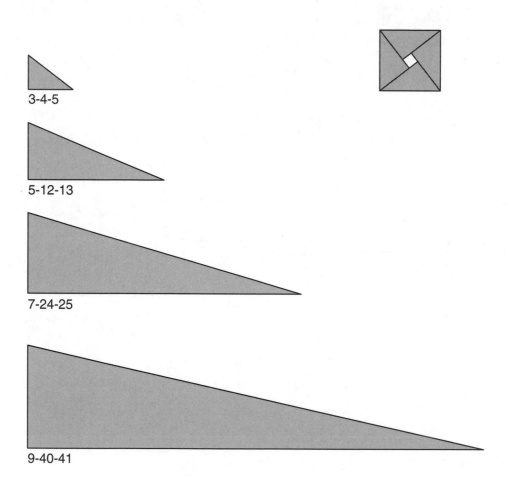

3-4-5

5-12-13

7-24-25

9-40-41

Mathematical Quilts—No Sewing Required!

ACTIVITY 3

Right Triangle Triples

A set of right triangle triples consists of three numbers that can be the measures for the sides of a right triangle. Although it's possible for the sides of right triangles to have noninteger lengths, in this activity you will work with triples that are all integers.

A right triangle whose legs are 3 and 4 units in length and whose hypotenuse is 5 units in length is perhaps the best-known right triangle. In fact, this combination is the only set of three consecutive integers that fits the $a^2 + b^2 = c^2$ relationship.

a. Below are some right triangle triples. Look for patterns, and fill in the missing number in each set of triples. Describe any patterns you find.

Some sets of right triangle triples		
3	4	5
5		13
7	24	
9		41

b. What would be the side lengths of the next right triangle if you continued to follow the pattern in the table?

Pythagoras Meets Fibonacci

Charles Raine described an interesting theorem that relates Pythagorean right triangle triples and the Fibonacci sequence. He stated that if you take any four consecutive Fibonacci numbers, the product of the outer terms and two times the product of the inner terms are the legs of a right triangle whose hypotenuse is also a Fibonacci number. For example, the Fibonacci sequence 3, 5, 8, 13 gives the two legs, 39 and 80, of a right triangle. And the hypotenuse of this triangle is 89, which is also a Fibonacci number! This Fibonacci number, 89, is the eleventh term in the sequence, so its subscript is 11, which is half the sum of the subscripts of the four original numbers $[(4 + 5 + 6 + 7) \div 2]$. Finally, the area of the triangle is the product of the original four numbers, 1560.

a. Show that Charles Raine's theorem works for each sequence of these four consecutive Fibonacci numbers:

$$8, 13, 21, 34 \qquad 13, 21, 34, 55$$

b. Choose another set of four consecutive Fibonacci numbers, and show that Raine's theorem works.

c. Use algebra to show why the theorem works.

Mathematical Quilts—No Sewing Required!
©1999 Key Curriculum Press

Generating Right Triangle Triples

Pythagorean triples can be generated using a variety of rules. Below are four different rules that have been used to find sets of right triangle triples.

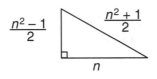

Rule of Pythagoras

n is any odd number

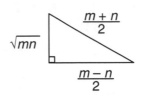

Rule of Euclid

m and *n* are both odd or both even, *m* > *n*, and the product, *mn*, must be a square number

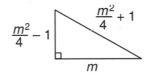

Rule of Plato

m is any even number

Rule of Masères

m and *n* can be any two integers and *m* > *n*

a. Choose values for *m* and *n*, and show that each set of rules does indeed generate sets of right triangle triples.

b. Use algebra to prove that each rule generates sets of right triangle triples.

Proofs of the Right Triangle $a^2 + b^2 = c^2$ Relationship

There are over 300 proofs of the Pythagorean theorem. A former president of the United States, James Garfield, even wrote an original proof of this theorem. Find two different proofs of the theorem, and share your proofs with your classmates.

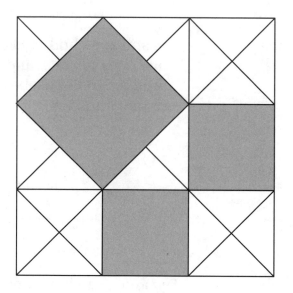

Pythagorean Triangle Relationships

Waclaw Sierpiński, in his book *Pythagorean Triangles,* describes and proves many relationships in Pythagorean triangles. Some of these relationships are given below. Choose any two of these relationships, describe each relationship in your own words, and give examples of triangles that satisfy each relationship.

1. All primitive Pythagorean triangles (x, y, z) in which y is an even number can be obtained from the formulas:

$$x = m^2 - n^2, \quad y = 2mn, \quad \text{and} \quad z = m^2 + n^2$$

where $m > n$ and m, n is all pairs of relatively prime numbers of which one is even and the other odd.

2. There are no Pythagorean triangles all of whose sides are prime numbers.

3. There are no Pythagorean triangles in which at least two sides are square numbers. There are Pythagorean triangles in which the hypotenuse and one leg are prime numbers. We do not know if there are infinitely many sets of these triangles.

4. For each natural number n, there exist at least n noncongruent Pythagorean triangles with the same perimeter.

5. Each Pythagorean triangle has an area that is a natural number divisible by 6. In each Pythagorean triangle, at least one of the legs is divisible by 4 and at least one is divisible by 3, so their product is divisible by 12.

6. The smallest pair of Pythagorean triangles with different hypotenuses and the same area are the 20-21-29 and 12-35-37 triangles.

A Logarithmic Spiral?

In a logarithmic spiral, the ratios of consecutive radii are constant.
Measure each radii in the design below, and determine whether
this spiral approximates a logarithmic spiral.

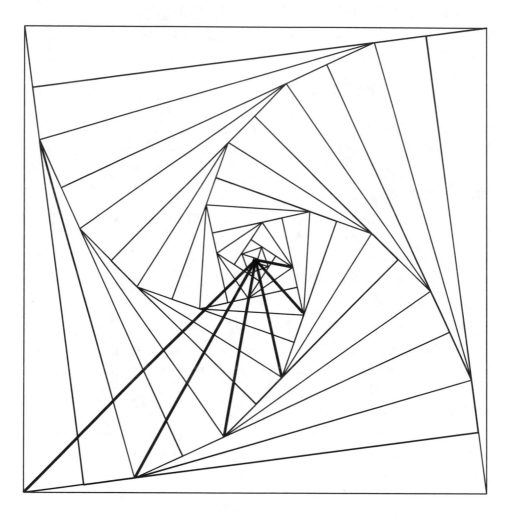

Primitive Right Triangle Triples

Sets of right triangle triples in which a and b are relatively prime—that is, their greatest common divisor is 1—are called *primitive* triples. For example, the pairs (3, 4) and (5, 12) are relatively prime because 1 is their only common divisor. For some of the primitive triples, b and c are consecutive integers. Primitive sets of triples can also be derived by choosing two numbers, m and n, and substituting them in the formulas below. Choose values for m and n such that they are relatively prime and either m or n is even and the other is odd.

$$a = m^2 - n^2, \quad b = 2mn, \quad \text{and} \quad c = m^2 + n^2$$

a. Using these formulas, start with $m = 2$ and $n = 1$ to generate a table of right triangle triples.

Pythagorean Triples

m	n	a	b	c	abc
2	1				
3	2				
4	1				
4	3				
7	6				

b. Describe any common characteristics of the right triangle triples in the table.

c. Find the product of a, b, and c for the first six sets of right triangle triples. Describe any patterns or common characteristics.

Graphing Calculator Explorations

Enter the program below on a TI-82 or TI-83 calculator to generate
sets of primitive right triangle triples. Both of these programs will
run until you press ⎡ON⎤ or the calculator runs out of memory. After
you quit the program, you can see the list of triples generated by
looking at L1, L2, and L3. If you want to generate a specific number
of triples—for example, 47 sets—change the Lbl 1 command to
"Repeat J=47" and the Goto 1 command to "End." Either of these
programs will produce 100 sets of triples in less than a minute.

TI-83	TI-82
1→U:0→J	1→U:0→J
Lbl 1	Lbl 1
U+1→U	U+1→U
For(V,3-gcd(U,2),U-1,2)	For(V,1+2fPart(U/2),U-1,2)
If gcd(U,V)=1:Then	V→W
U²-V²→A	While fPart(U/W)>0 or
2UV→B	fPart(U/W)>0
U²+V²→C	W-1→W
J+1→J:A→L₁(J)	End
B→L₂(J):C→L₃(J)	If W=1:Then
Disp {A,B,C}	U²-V²→A
End	2UV→B
End	U²+V²→C
Goto 1	J+1→J:A→L₁(J)
	B→L₂(J):C→L₃(J)
	Disp {A,B,C}
	End
	End
	Goto 1

ACTIVITY 11

Internet Explorations

This Web site will provide you with a lot of information about
Pythagorean triples. Discover something you didn't know before,
and prepare a short presentation on what you learned.

`http://mathworld.wolfram.com/PythagoreanTriple.html`

The Behold! Quilt

The pattern for the Behold! quilt is based on a picture proof of the Pythagorean theorem and is made up of 16 identical squares. Each square is formed by tessellating four congruent right triangles, in this case the 3-4-5 right triangle, around a center square, with the four hypotenuses forming the newly created square. This square is also the beginning of the pattern for the two Pythagorean triples quilts.

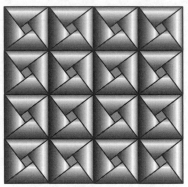

An interesting phenomenon happens when you place 16 Behold! squares in a 4 × 4 grid. The hypotenuses of the right triangles form the sides of the squares. Notice that the adjacent triangles are 180° rotations of each other. Each individual square has its own design, but when the squares are arranged in a larger design, another pattern of rectangles emerges. This new, larger design is an example of the synergy that often occurs in quilt patterns.

Designing Your Quilt

1. To create the design for the Behold! quilt, follow these steps:

   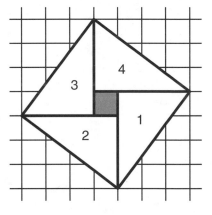

   Step 1 Start by drawing a small square on graph paper. The length you use for the side length of the square will be the unit measure for the triangles. If you start with a side length other than 1, you will have to adjust the side lengths of your 3-4-5 triangle accordingly.

   Step 2 Surround the square with four 3-4-5 triangles.

   Step 3 Make 15 more of these squares.

   Step 4 Cut out the 16 squares and arrange them in a 4 × 4 grid.

2. Many other quilt patterns using squares are possible. The square shown at the right is the basis of many quilt patterns. Notice that the square is divided into two right triangles formed by the diagonal. One of the triangles is shaded.

   a. Cut out the squares on the Quilt Design Worksheet page. Also included on this page are six solid shaded squares and six unshaded squares.

   b. Experiment with creating patterns by arranging the squares.

   c. When you have found a pattern that you like, either glue the squares onto paper or draw the design on graph paper, adding other colors if you like.

   d. Compare your design with those of your classmates.

   e. Comment on the synergy of the designs. What shapes and patterns were formed?

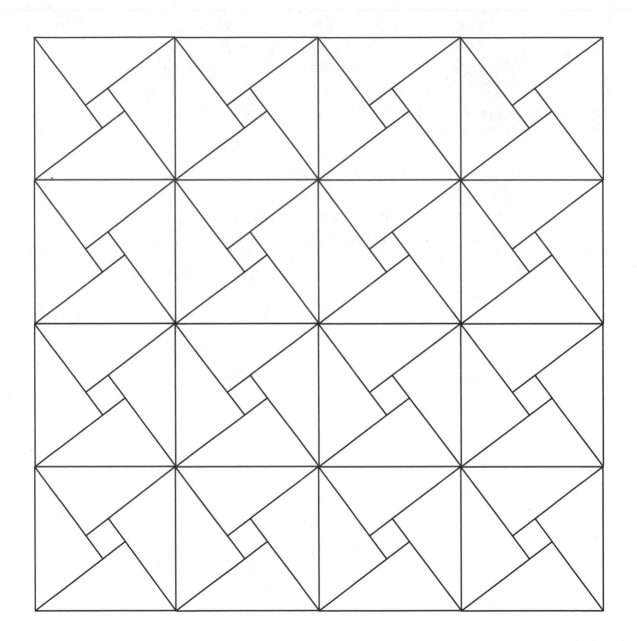

Mathematical Quilts—No Sewing Required!
©1999 Key Curriculum Press

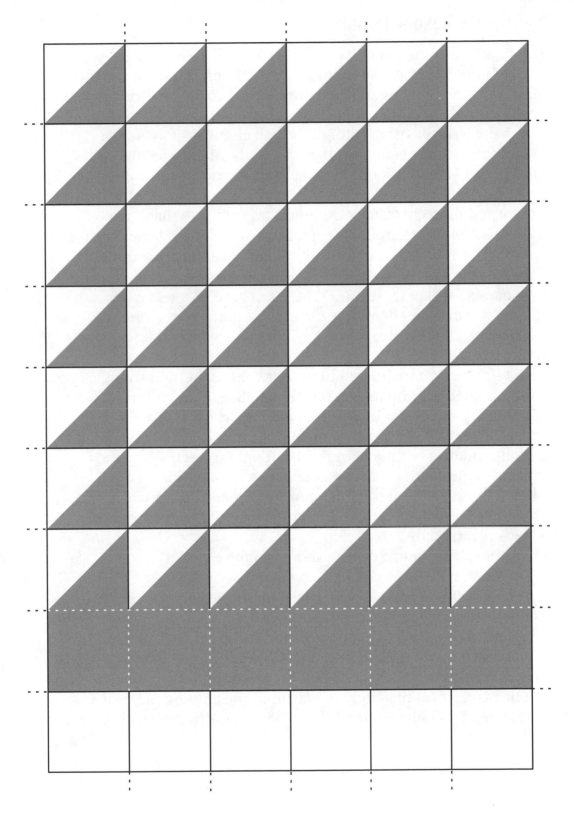

Making the Behold! Quilt

The final size of the Behold! quilt is $23'' \times 23''$. You will need $\frac{1}{4}$ yard each of four colors for the triangles if you choose solid colors. The quilt designer chose an unusual print for the triangle fabric, however, and needed 1 yard of each fabric color in order to cut from selected areas of the fabric. You will also need $1\frac{1}{2}$ yards of black fabric for the centers of the squares, borders, backing, and binding, and an additional $\frac{1}{8}$ yard of color fabric for the border.

Creating this quilt requires only two polygonal shapes—the center square and the right triangle. Although any of the Pythagorean triples will tessellate around a center square to form a larger square pattern, the 3-4-5 series permits the smallest center square and a right triangle with two relatively large acute angles. The other Pythagorean triples (5-12-13, 7-24-25, . . .) have a larger center square, which might dominate the triangle pattern, and one very small acute angle, which would be difficult to work with in fabric.

The Behold! quilt is constructed from 16 identical squares. Each of the squares is constructed from four congruent right triangles hand-stitched around the center square. (See the discussion of the Spiraling Pythagorean Triples quilt for construction of a similar square.) The unit of construction for this quilt is 1 inch. The quilt designer made a template for the 3-4-5 right triangle using those exact measurements. The center square template was a 1-inch square. Because these squares were hand-pieced, a $\frac{1}{4}$-inch seam allowance was added after the templates were traced onto the fabric's reverse side.

For the fabric for this design, shown on the cover of this book, Nancy Crow's graded-colors fabrics were selected for their visual appeal. However, these fabrics were already divided into isosceles triangles, so a template of the 3-4-5 triangle was constructed to use as much of the isosceles triangles as possible. The accompanying diagram shows how the template can be placed over the fabric to maximize the amount of fabric for the design. Quilters often have to be creative in their use of

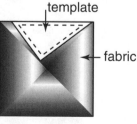

template

fabric

geometry to make a quilt pattern fit the design of a chosen fabric. In this case, the quilt designer used a knowledge of similar 3-4-5 triangles.

Next, the 16 Behold! squares were stitched together, matching adjacent colored triangles. After a border was added, the finished quilt top was layered with a lightweight batting and cotton backing, and machine-quilted along the lines of the squares. A black binding identical to the black border fabric completed the quilt.

The Pythagorean Triples Quilt

The design for this quilt was based on the June 1989 cover of *Mathematics Magazine*, published by the Mathematical Association of America. In this quilt, the four 3-4-5 triangles are nested next to the 1×1 initiating square. Four more 3-4-5 triangles are rotated and positioned so that their hypotenuses are adjacent to the original hypotenuses. What is fascinating is the fact that the 5-12-13 triangles can then be nested next to the 3-4-5 triangles, followed by the 7-24-25 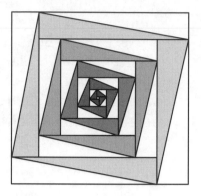 triangles, which nest next to the 5-12-13 triangles, and so on. You can continue this process indefinitely. The sides of the right triangles in this quilt are 3-4-5, 5-12-13, 7-24-25, 9-40-41, and 11-60-61. Notice the rectangles that are formed by rotating each triangle 180° about the midpoint of its hypotenuse. In this sense, the quilt design was fixed before the quilt was started. However, you should experiment with various-sized right triangles to form a pleasing pattern. The Spiraling Pythagorean Triples quilt uses the same triangles as this quilt.

Designing Your Quilt

Creating the design for this quilt is like putting together pieces of a puzzle. Follow these steps to create your design:

Step 1 On graph paper, draw patterns for each of these triangles:

3-4-5, 5-12-13, 7-24-25, 9-40-41

Step 2 Trace around your patterns, and cut out four copies of each triangle from your choice of colored paper and four copies of each triangle from white paper.

Step 3 Start with the smallest set of colored triangles. Arrange them so that they form a square, with a 1-unit square in the center.

Step 4 Now place the smallest white triangles around the square of colored triangles to create another square.

Step 5 Continue in the same manner with the next-larger-size colored square. Then add a round of the same-sized white triangles. Each time you add four triangles, you should get another square.

Step 6 When you are satisfied with your design, glue it to a large piece of paper or to tagboard.

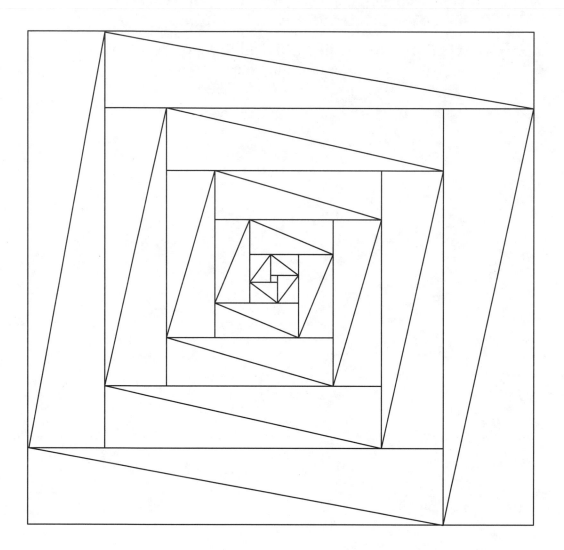

Mathematical Quilts—No Sewing Required!

Making the Pythagorean Triples Quilt

The finished size of this quilt is 37" × 37". You'll need $1\frac{1}{4}$ yards of fabric for the backing and $\frac{3}{4}$ yard of fabric for the border. Be sure to cut the border on the bias. You will also need scraps or about $\frac{1}{8}$ yard of 50 different fabrics for the design if you make the triangles out of individual squares as shown in this quilt. To construct this quilt, the designer strip-pieced the small $\frac{1}{2}$-inch squares of each triangle together.

Even though the original quilt was strip-pieced together without a foundation, you might want to use a foundation for piecing, such as freezer paper or muslin. Another technique for sewing this quilt that might be faster is to sew all the small squares together and then appliqué the white triangles on top of the pieced squares.

The quilt starts with the unit square at the center. Around the 1-inch square, sew four 3-4-5 triangles, keeping the longer leg adjacent to the inner square. Although you can sew the first three triangles together quite easily, the fourth triangle may require some hand stitching. At this point, the original 1 × 1 square will be surrounded by a square that measures 5 units to a side. Now sew the white 3-4-5 triangles onto the hypotenuses of the checkered triangles. This new square will measure 7 units to a side.

Continue to add layers of the 5-12-13 triangles, the 7-24-25 triangles, the 9-40-41 triangles, and finally the 11-60-61 triangles. You can stop adding triangles at almost any point. The quilt designer originally planned to use a larger set of triangles but stopped with the 11-60-61 triangles because that size was already quite difficult to work with.

After you have pieced the top of the quilt, add cotton batting and complete the quilting using a stitch-in-the-ditch technique. Once you have bound your quilt, you might want to add a tubular sleeve on the back. Even though this quilt is not large, the extra fabric from the seam allowances becomes a problem, because the weight of the extra material will tend to make the large triangles sag. One suggestion is to back these pieces with an interfacing before assembling the quilt.

The Spiraling Pythagorean Triples Quilt

Spirals are the basis for many quilt patterns. The design for the Spiraling Pythagorean Triples quilt is formed by tessellating four congruent right triangles around a center square to form a larger square. Each triangle is then reflected on its hypotenuse to form another larger square. Successively larger triangles are arranged around each square to form a larger square and then reflected around the growing center square to form the spiral pattern. This design was inspired by the cover of the June 1989 *Mathematics Magazine,* published by the Mathematical Association of America, and the accompanying article, "A Pythagorean Tiling of the Plane," by Ernest Eckert and Hugo Haagensen. The Pythagorean triples that will form a spiral are those in which the sum of the measures of the legs equals the difference in the measures of the legs of the next right triangle. For example, if the first triangle is a 3-4-5 triangle, then the next triangle must be a 5-12-13 triangle because $3 + 4 = 12 - 5$.

The set of triangles used for this spiral is a unique set of right triangle triples in which sides a are consecutive odd integers and sides b and c are consecutive integers. The table at right lists the triples used for the quilt.

Pythagorean Triples

a	b	c
3	4	5
5	12	13
7	24	25
9	40	41
11	60	61
13	84	85
15	112	113

The visual appeal of this pattern of triangles and reflections, in addition to the tessellation, stems from its spiraling design. As the lengths of the hypotenuse (c) and longer leg (b) become larger, the four short legs spiral outward to each of the four corners of the finished square and give the illusion of a curve. This spiral is similar to the logarithmic spiral in the Indiana Puzzle quilt. However, because the ratios of succeeding triangles are not constant, it is not a true logarithmic spiral.

The quilt's designer used solid-colored fabrics in shades of the spectrum for the tessellating triangles in this quilt. For the reflections, a solid black fabric was used.

Designing Your Quilt

1. Follow these steps to create the design for the Spiraling Pythagorean Triples quilt:

   Step 1   On graph paper, draw patterns for each of these triangles:

   > 3-4-5, 5-12-13, 7-24-25, 9-40-41,
   > 11-60-61, 13-84-85, 15-112-113

   Step 2   Mark each pattern piece on one side with a 1 and on the other side with a 2.

   Step 3   With side 1 facing up, trace around your patterns, and cut out four copies of each triangle from your choice of colored paper.

   Step 4   With side 2 facing up, trace around your patterns, and cut out four copies of each triangle from black paper.

   Step 5   Start with the smallest set of colored triangles. Arrange them so that they form a square with a 1-unit square in the center.

   Step 6   Now arrange the smallest black triangles around the square of colored triangles so that each black triangle is a reflection of the colored triangle along the hypotenuse.

Step 7   Arrange the next-larger-size colored triangles around the new square so that the right angles of the smaller triangles and the right angles of the larger triangles share a common vertex. Then add a round of the same-sized black triangles, reflecting them as you did in Step 6. Each time you add four triangles, the result should be another square.

Step 8   When you are satisfied with your design, glue it to a large piece of paper or to tagboard.

2. Create a quilt design based on an alpha spiral. See Activity 10 for directions on how to draw an alpha spiral.

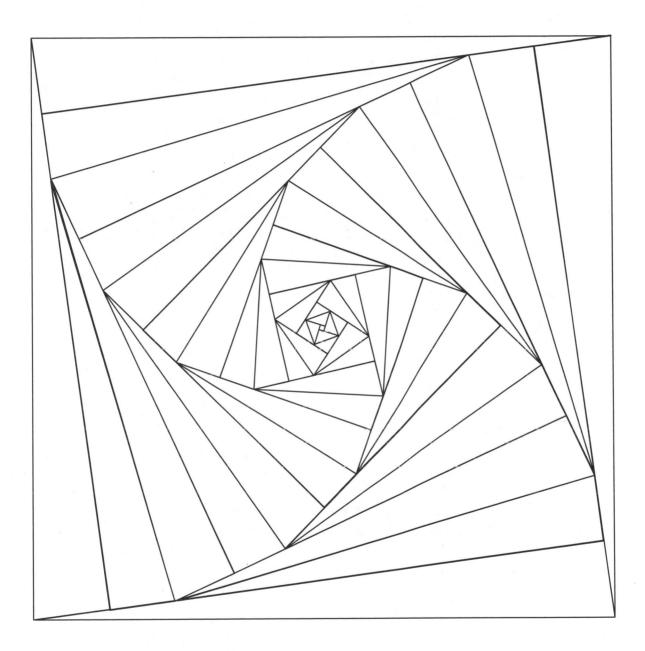

Making the Spiraling Pythagorean Triples Quilt

The unit of measure for this quilt is $\frac{1}{4}$ inch. Although this unit was a small and difficult one to work with for the center square and triangles, it kept the dimensions of the finished quilt reasonable. The largest triangle is the 13-84-85, which translated to 3.25-21-21.25 inches. The center square used to begin this quilt was $\frac{1}{4}$ inch on each side. The next level was composed of triangles whose sides measured $\frac{3}{4}$ inch, 1 inch, and $1\frac{1}{4}$ inch. The finished size of the quilt was $32\frac{1}{2}$ inches square.

The designer used solid-color cotton fabrics to make this quilt. Templates for the triangles were cut from plastic with a $\frac{1}{4}$-inch grid, to the finished measure of each triangle. Dimensions for each triangle are given in the table below. You will need 1 yard of the black fabric; scraps or fat quarters for the purple, blue, and aqua fabrics; and $\frac{1}{4}$ yard of the green, yellow, orange, and red fabrics.

Color	a	b	c
4 purple and 4 black	1.25″	1.5″	1.75″
4 blue and 4 black	1.75″	3.5″	3.75″
4 aqua and 4 black	2.25″	6.5″	6.75″
4 green and 4 black	2.75″	10.5″	10.75″
4 yellow and 4 black	3.25″	15.5″	15.75″
4 orange and 4 black	3.75″	21.5″	21.75″
4 red and 4 black	4.25″	28.5″	28.75″

Trace around the template onto the fabric using a pencil or colored chalk. Add a $\frac{1}{4}$-inch seam allowance on each side of the triangle. Machine- or hand-stitch on the traced line. After you cut all the pieces, begin sewing from the center of the design. Stitch a purple 3-4-5 triangle to the unit square, matching seam lines. Add the second, third, and fourth triangles in a similar manner. Press the seams in one direction, and sew the four black 3-4-5 triangles to the preceding square, spiraling as the drafting pattern illustrates. Continue with each color and its reflection. End with a black triangle.

Mathematical Quilts—No Sewing Required!

Because the hypotenuse is cut on the bias of the fabric, it tends to stretch in sewing. Using the traced seam line as a guide, pin each seam for its full length before stitching. Pressing with a steam iron will shrink most of the stretching that occurs during sewing. The new $\frac{1}{4}$-inch-grid iron-on paper template material now available makes machine construction of this quilt possible. (See the directions for the Indiana Puzzle quilt.)

The finished square should measure approximately 32.5 inches on each side. Layer it with batting and backing, and baste the three layers together. Quilt along the seam lines or add decorative quilting within the triangles. Bind off the perimeter of the quilt with black fabric, and add a rod pocket for hanging.

TEACHER NOTES

The activities in this section focus on right triangle triples and the idea of synergy in design. The Behold! quilt is based on Bhāskara's picture proof of the right triangle relationship $a^2 + b^2 = c^2$. The Pythagorean Triples quilt is based on an interesting pattern that is formed when you arrange increasingly larger right triangles around a center square. The same set of right triangles is used for both the Pythagorean Triples quilt and the Spiraling Pythagorean Triples quilt. For both quilts, you start with the 3-4-5 triangle. All of the triangles have two common characteristics—the first number in the triple is odd and the last two numbers are consecutive integers. Your students will be fascinated by the effects they can achieve by arranging the triangles in a slightly different fashion.

In Activity 1, students explain why Bhāskara's diagram represents a "proof" of the right triangle relationship $a^2 + b^2 = c^2$. This diagram is the basic unit of the Behold! quilt. In Activity 2, they experiment to see if any set of four right triangles can be arranged to form a square, as in Bhāskara's proof. The algebra that forms the basis for the design of the Behold! quilt will complement any lesson on the Pythagorean theorem. Students should find it interesting that early mathematicians used algebra to prove geometry and geometry to visually represent algebra; connections between these two branches of mathematics are often overlooked in traditional curriculums.

In Activities 3, 5, 7, and 9, students explore right triangle triples in a variety of ways. In Activity 9, the terms *primitive right triangle triples* and *relatively prime* are defined. Students should have calculators available for the computations needed for many of the activities in this section so that they can concentrate on looking for patterns, and not on doing computations.

Activity 4 presents an interesting relationship between right triangle triples and the Fibonacci sequence. In Activity 6, students research other proofs of the right triangle relationship. In Activity 8, they investigate a spiral formed by right triangles to see if it is a logarithmic spiral. (More information related to logarithmic spirals is presented in the Spiral Quilts section.)

Answers and Comments

Activity 1

$$c^2 = (b - a)^2 + 4\left(\tfrac{1}{2}ab\right)$$
$$= b^2 - 2ab + a^2 - 2ab$$
$$= b^2 + a^2$$
$$= a^2 + b^2$$

Activity 2

This process will work with any right triangle because you place the triangles together in such a way that the two complementary acute angles always share a common vertex, which means the sum of these angles is 90°. The side length of the square in the center is the difference between the long leg and the short leg. The side length of the outer square is the same as the length of the hypotenuse of the triangle.

Activity 3

a.

Some sets of right triangle triples

3	4	5
5	12	13
7	24	25
9	40	41

b. Students may note that the shortest leg in each triangle is a consecutive odd integer. If you take the lengths of the short and long legs for the previous triangle and add them together, and then add the length of the new short leg, you get the length of the long leg for the new triangle. To predict the length of the hypotenuse, add 1 to the length of the longer leg.

TEACHER NOTES

Upper-level students can try expressing this pattern with symbols. If a represents the shorter leg, b the longer leg, and c the hypotenuse, then

$$a_{n+1} = a_n + 2$$
$$b_{n+1} = a_{n+1} + a_n + b_n$$
$$c_{n+1} = \left(a_{n+1}\right)^2 + \left(b_{n+1}\right)^2 \quad \text{or} \quad c_{n+1} = b_{n+1} + 1$$

With these patterns, students can generate larger and larger triples.

Activity 4

a. $(8)(34) = 272$ and $2(13)(21) = 546$, so the hypotenuse would be $\sqrt{272^2 + 546^2} = 610$, which is the fifteenth Fibonacci number.

$13(55) = 715$ and $2(21)(34) = 1428$, so the hypotenuse would be $\sqrt{715^2 + 1428^2} = 1597$, which is the seventeenth Fibonacci number.

b. Answers will vary.

c. William Boulger provides two proofs of this relationship. The first is a simple algebraic exercise; the second, and more rigorous, approach uses number theory and mathematical induction. The algebraic approach is shown here.

Let the four consecutive Fibonacci numbers be denoted by a, b, $a + b$, and $a + 2b$. The first leg of the right triangle would be represented by $a(a + 2b)$ or $a^2 + 2ab$. The second leg would be represented by $2[b(a + b)]$ or $2ab + 2b^2$. Therefore,

$$
\begin{aligned}
\left(a^2 + 2ab\right)^2 + \left(2ab + 2b^2\right)^2 &= a^4 + 4a^3b + 4a^2b^2 + 4a^2b^2 + 8ab^3 + 4b^4 \\
&= a^4 + 4a^3b + 8a^2b^2 + 8ab^3 + 4b^4 \\
&= \left(a^2 + 2ab + 2b^2\right)^2
\end{aligned}
$$

The expression $a^2 + 2ab + 2b^2$ represents the hypotenuse. Because $a^2 + 2ab + 2b^2$ can be rewritten as $b^2 + (a + b)^2$, we know that the hypotenuse of the right triangle is the sum of the squares of the two middle Fibonacci numbers.

To show that the area of the right triangle is the product of the four original Fibonacci numbers, simplify and rearrange the expression for the area of the triangle.

$$\text{Area} = \tfrac{1}{2}\left(a^2 + 2ab\right)\left(2ab + b^2\right)$$
$$= \left(a^2 + 2ab\right)\left(ab + b^2\right)$$
$$= (a)(a + 2b)(b)(a + b)$$
$$= ab(a + b)(a + 2b)$$

$a^2 + 2ab$

$2ab + 2b^2$

Activity 5

a. Answers will vary.

b. Rule of Pythagoras:

Show that
$$\left(\frac{n^2 - 1}{2}\right)^2 + n^2 = \left(\frac{n^2 + 1}{2}\right)^2$$
$$\left(\frac{n^4 - 2n^2 + 1}{4}\right) + n^2 = \left(\frac{n^4 + 2n^2 + 1}{4}\right)$$
$$n^4 - 2n^2 + 1 + 4n^2 = n^4 + 2n^2 + 1$$
$$n^4 + 2n^2 + 1 = n^4 + 2n^2 + 1$$

Rule of Euclid:

Show that
$$\left(\sqrt{mn}\right)^2 + \left(\frac{m - n}{2}\right)^2 = \left(\frac{m + n}{2}\right)^2$$
$$mn + \left(\frac{m^2 - 2mn + n^2}{4}\right) = \left(\frac{m^2 + 2mn + n^2}{2}\right)$$
$$4mn + m^2 - 2mn + n^2 = m^2 + 2mn + n^2$$
$$m^2 + 2mn + n^2 = m^2 + 2mn + n^2$$

Rule of Plato:

Show that
$$\left(\frac{m^2}{4} - 1\right)^2 + m^2 = \left(\frac{m^2}{4} + 1\right)^2$$
$$\frac{m^4}{16} - \frac{m^2}{2} + 1 + m^2 = \frac{m^4}{16} + \frac{m^2}{2} + 1 + m^2$$
$$\frac{m^4}{16} + \frac{m^2}{2} + 1 = \frac{m^4}{16} + \frac{m^2}{2} + 1$$

Rule of Masères:

Show that
$$\left(2mn\right)^2 + \left(m^2 - n^2\right)^2 = \left(m^2 + n^2\right)^2$$
$$4m^2n^2 + m^4 - 2m^2n^2 + n^4 = m^4 + 2m^2n^2 + n^4$$
$$m^4 + 2m^2n^2 + n^4 = m^4 + 2m^2n^2 + n^4$$

Activity 6

Answers will vary.

Activity 7

Answers will vary.

TEACHER NOTES

Activity 8

The sequence of ratios is approximately 1.82, 1.65, 1.52, 1.4, 1.29, so the spiral is not a true logarithmic spiral. However, it is a close approximation of one.

Activity 9

a.

m	n	a	b	c	abc
2	1	3	4	5	60
3	2	5	12	13	780
4	1	15	8	17	2040
4	3	7	24	25	4200
5	2	21	20	29	12,180
5	4	9	40	41	14,760
6	1	35	12	37	15,540
6	5	11	60	61	40,260
7	6	13	84	85	92,820

b. Answers may vary. Each set of triples contains two odd numbers and one even number.

c. Answers may vary. The products are all multiples of 10. They are also increasing.

Activity 10

Answers will vary.

Activity 11

Answers will vary.

Resources and Selected Readings

Armstrong, James W. *Elements of Mathematics,* 2d ed. New York: Macmillan, 1976.

Boulger, William. "Pythagoras Meets Fibonacci." Pp. 277–82 in *The Mathematics Teacher.* Reston, VA: NCTM Publications, 1989.

Eves, Howard. *An Introduction to the History of Mathematics,* 4th ed. New York: Holt, Rinehart & Winston, 1976.

Huntley, H. E. *The Divine Proportion.* New York: Dover, 1970.

Mathematical Association of America. *Mathematics Magazine,* Vol. 62, No. 3, June 1989.

O'Daffer, Phares G., and Stanley R. Clemens. *Geometry: An Investigative Approach,* 2d ed. Reading, MA: Addison-Wesley, 1992.

Posamentier, Alfred S., and Jay Stepelman. *Teaching Secondary School Mathematics,* 3d ed. Columbus, OH: Merrill, 1981.

Sierpiński, Waclaw. *Pythagorean Triangles.* New York: Graduate School of Science, Yeshiva University, 1962.

Smith, Sanderson. *Agnesi to Zeno: Over 100 Vignettes from the History of Mathematics.* Berkeley, CA: Key Curriculum Press, 1996.

The Tiling Quilts

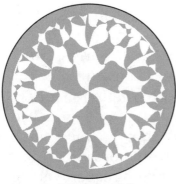

The Poincaré Plane Quilt

TESSELLATIONS, OR PATTERNS OF ONE OR MORE polygons that completely cover a surface without any open space or overlapping, have been part of the decorative arts of many cultures. The ancient Sumerians (circa 4000 B.C.) used geometric mosaic tile patterns in floors and on walls, often by tessellating several polygons. Later (circa A.D. 700–1500), Moorish artists used geometric designs and tessellations as ornamental patterns for floors, walls, fabrics, and other artwork because the Islamic religion prohibited art that represented people, animals, or other real-world objects. Throughout history, mathematicians and artists have explored polygonal shapes that will tessellate by themselves or in combination with other polygons.

Quilters have learned which shapes tessellate. Most pieced quilts, particularly those made by sewing small shapes into larger designs, are tessellations.

The Tessellating Tetrominoes Quilt

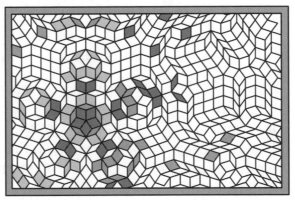

The Penrose Tiles Quilt

The shapes most commonly used by quilters are the square, the equilateral triangle, and the regular hexagon.

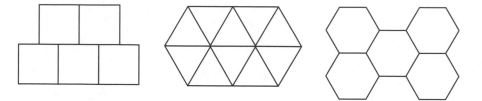

Quilters often create designs that fit into squares and then join the squares to make the quilt. Often, when squares are combined with other, similar squares, an even more complex pattern emerges. The Indiana Puzzle quilt is an example of this synergy of design.

The Tessellating Tetrominoes quilt is a tiling of tetromino shapes based on the computer game Tetris™. The tiles in this quilt are called tetrominoes because they are formations of four squares. These tiles belong to a special family of polygons called polyominoes. All of the shapes in this polyomino family are made from joining squares along congruent sides. A monomino is one square (mono = one), a shape that will always tessellate itself. Think of rooms whose floors or ceilings are covered with square tiles. Dominoes are formed from two squares. You may be familiar with dominoes, a popular game played with two-squared tiles with numbers on each tile. Trominoes are formed from three squares, tetrominoes from four squares, pentominoes from five squares, and so on.

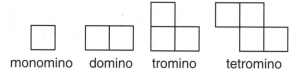

monomino   domino   tromino   tetromino

Probably, the tiling patterns you are most familiar with are periodic tilings—tilings that cover the plane in a repeating pattern that has translational symmetry. Aperiodic tiling patterns do not have translational symmetry—that is, sliding, or translating, the design does not replicate the pattern. The Penrose Tiles quilt was designed using what are called Penrose tiles, a special set of tiles that tile the plane aperiodically.

Mathematical Quilts—No Sewing Required!
©1999 Key Curriculum Press

Problems related to tiling the plane date back to the ancient Greeks. And today mathematicians are still interested in tiling patterns, particularly sets of tiles that tile the plane in an aperiodic fashion, that is, a tiling in which there is no apparent regular pattern. In 1964, Robert Berger proposed a set of 20,000 tiles that would tile a plane in an aperiodic fashion. However, the ultimate quest among mathematicians became to tile the plane with sets containing the fewest number of tiles. Sometime later, Raphael Robinson reduced the set of tiles to six.

In 1974, Roger Penrose, a British mathematical physicist, discovered a set of two tiles that would cover the plane in an aperiodic fashion. These tiles became known as Penrose tiles. This first set of Penrose tiles, called darts and kites, was derived from the pentagon.

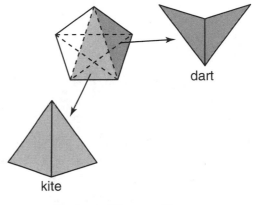

First set of Penrose tiles

The dart and kite can fit together to form a rhombus that will tile the plane periodically.

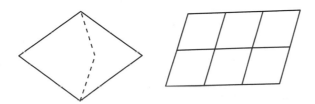

For the tiles to cover the plane in an aperiodic fashion, the rules needed to be defined for joining the two tiles. Penrose discovered that the darts and kites could nest in an aperiodic fashion if the sides were divided into a Golden Ratio relationship. To illustrate that idea, notice the lighter and darker arcs in the figures below. If you use the rule of matching the arcs—lighter with lighter and darker with darker—the dart and kite become aperiodic tiles.

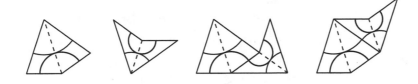

In 1979, Penrose discovered another set of aperiodic tiles, which are often called "fat" and "skinny" rhombuses. The fat rhombus is formed by combining a kite and a dart. This rhombus has angles of 72° and 108°. The skinny rhombus is formed by joining two Golden Triangles together at their bases. The skinny rhombus has angles of 36° and 144°. The rule for tiling with these rhombuses is to match tiles according to corresponding arrows, as shown here.

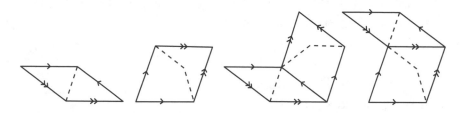

Any Penrose tiling can be constructed in an infinite number of ways. The intrigue lies in the fact that every pattern will be aperiodic. You can even generalize these tilings to three dimensions, using solid polyhedrons that fill space without gaps. The three-dimensional tilings are also aperiodic.

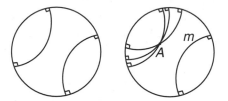

The third tiling quilt explores the Poincaré plane, which was named after French mathematician Henri Poincaré (1854–1912). Poincaré constructed a model of hyperbolic geometry in which the Euclidean plane is replaced by the interior of a circle. Straight lines are represented by the arcs of the circle, which, when extended, meet the edge of the circle at right angles (orthogonally). The edge of the circle can be thought of as the infinitely distant edge.

The major focus of Euclidean geometry is the parallel postulate, which states that for any point not on a given line, there is one and only one line that passes through the point and is parallel to the given line. In the Poincaré model, there is more than one line parallel to a given line through a given point not on the line.

Mathematical Quilts—No Sewing Required!
©1999 Key Curriculum Press

The idea of congruence in Poincaré's model is also different from what is stated in Euclidean geometry. In the Poincaré plane quilt, all the bird-shaped figures are considered congruent, and there is no such thing as a scaled-down figure in this world. How can this make sense? The Poincaré circle is considered the "infinitely distant" edge of the "universe," and the sizes of the birds decrease as you walk from the center of the universe toward the "outer circle." As you walked "outwards," your footsteps, in the Euclidean view, would become smaller and smaller, so you would never be able to reach the edge of the circle. As an inhabitant of this new world, you would not be able to perceive change in size, because everything would constantly shrink or expand depending on which way you were moving—toward the center or toward the circumference of the circle.

There are some interesting connections between this quilt design and the work of Dutch artist M. C. Escher (1898–1972). Escher fabricated impossible three-dimensional objects and staircases that went nowhere. But he also experimented with regular divisions of the plane and the symmetry that developed from those divisions, and he made extensive use of grids. Sometimes, these grids were rectangular, like our Cartesian coordinate system. Other times, the grids were distorted, or more hyperbolic. If you study the grid of Escher's woodcut *Circle Limit 1,* you will see that the woodcut has what is called a P6 base group symmetry. This means that once the motif is established, in this case one-sixth of the circle, the motif is repeated after a rotation of 60°. (Jay Kappraff's book *Connections* has an excellent discussion of symmetry and symmetry groups.)

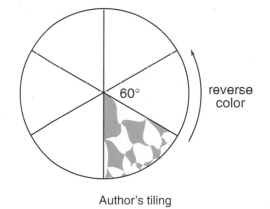

Author's tiling

The illustrations below show the similarities between the design Escher used for his *Circle Limit 1* woodcut and the design used for the quilt. Escher used triangles to tessellate the plane. The tessellating unit used for the quilt design was a quadrilateral.

Poincaré plane   Escher's *Circle Limit 1*   Poincaré plane quilt tiling

Designing a tiling quilt is fun! When creating designs for these quilts, feel free to experiment. Don't simply try to replicate the quilt designs as shown. Explore mathematics from a new and different perspective, and create a unique and personal quilt design.

Tessellating the Plane with Triangles and Quadrilaterals

Does every triangle tessellate a plane? Does every quadrilateral, convex or nonconvex, tessellate a plane? Investigate and then write a convincing argument to support your conclusions.

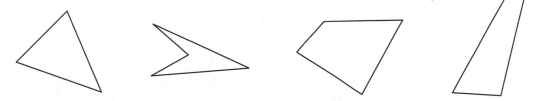

Tip: To experiment making tessellations on paper, draw a shape and trace it on tracing paper. Move the tracing paper so that you can trace a new piece adjacent to the original piece. Continue tracing pieces until you have tiled the plane. Another option is to cut a template out of tagboard and trace around this shape.

Polyomino Families

A polyomino is a polygon made of squares matched along an edge. Reflected and rotated shapes are considered to be the same.

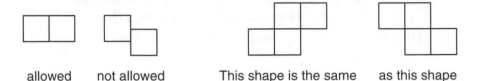

allowed   not allowed   This shape is the same   as this shape

You might want to use dot paper or graph paper for this activity.

1. Draw all of the shapes in each polyomino family: monomino, domino, and tromino. How many members are there in each family?

2. **a.** Find all possible tetromino shapes. Remember that edges must match, and assume that flipped or rotated forms of the same shape are the same.

   b. Draw the tetromino shapes that you found in part a, leaving room underneath each one for several transformations.

   c. Below each shape, draw a 90° rotation of the shape.

   d. Below each shape from part c, draw another 90° rotation of the shape.

   e. Draw two more 90° rotations for each shape.

   f. Which of the shapes did you find most difficult to visualize in their new positions? Compare the characteristics of shapes that are easy to visualize to those that are difficult to visualize. Consider qualities such as symmetry in your response.

   g. In designing the Tetris™ computer game for a two-dimensional screen, it was necessary to add pieces because you can't flip pieces on the screen. What two pieces had to be added?

Mathematical Quilts—No Sewing Required!
©1999 Key Curriculum Press

Tetromino Puzzles

You might want to use dot paper or graph paper for this activity.

1. Determine which of these tetromino shapes will tessellate themselves. Illustrate.

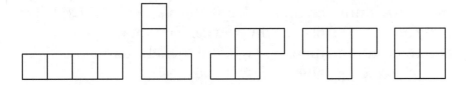

2. Choose at least two different tetromino shapes, and determine whether they will tessellate with each other. Illustrate.

3. Show how four T tetrominoes tessellate to form a square. Show how sixteen T tetrominoes tessellate to form a square.

4. A *reptile* is a polyomino that can tessellate to form larger versions of itself. The diagram below shows four tromino Ls forming a larger L. Show how nine tromino Ls can form an even larger L.

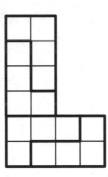

Penrose Tiles Vertex Nets

Make as many different symmetric shapes, or vertex nets, as you
can using only the tiles from one of the sets of Penrose tiles shown
below. You can use a tile more than once, but you cannot mix tiles
from the different sets. How many vertex nets did you find for
each set? Do you think you found all possible vertex nets? Explain
why or why not. (To do this activity, you can cut out the pieces
below and trace around them on tagboard to make templates.
Or you can use tracing paper and trace the tiles.)

 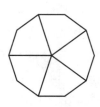

Set 1 tiles

 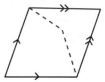

One possible vertex
net for set 1

Set 2 tiles

Mathematical Quilts—No Sewing Required!
©1999 Key Curriculum Press

ACTIVITY 5

A Special Relationship

A special relationship exists in both sets of Penrose tiles, the dart and the kite, and the "fat" and "skinny" rhombuses. Calculate the ratio of the areas of the two tiles in each set.

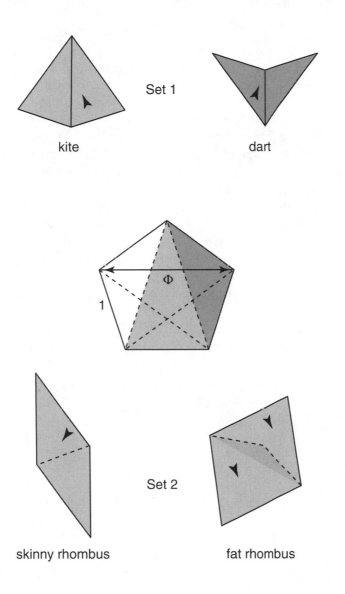

kite   Set 1   dart

skinny rhombus   Set 2   fat rhombus

Life on the Poincaré Plane

Below is a description of the Poincaré plane. Read it, and then write several paragraphs describing what it would be like to live on the Poincaré plane as compared to living in a three-dimensional Euclidean world. Use your imagination rather than precise mathematical terminology and definitions.

Close your eyes and imagine yourself living on the Poincaré plane. Your world is completely flat. At the "edges" of this world is a circular boundary—a boundary that is infinitely long. Begin walking from the center of this world to the outer edge. As you walk "outwards," your footsteps, in the Euclidean view, become smaller and smaller, so that you can never reach the edge of the circle. As an inhabitant of this new world, you cannot perceive change in size, because everything constantly shrinks or expands depending on which way you are moving—toward the center or toward the edge of the circle. When you walk along a straight line, you are actually traveling along an arc that can only meet the edge of the circular plane at a right angle. There are infinitely many parallel streets that pass through any point on the plane, giving you infinitely many options for travel in this world.

In your new world, all triangles are regular—that is, all sides and all angles are congruent, and the larger the triangle, the smaller the angles of the triangle become. In hyperbolic reality, all triangles are congruent. There is no such thing as a scaled-down figure in this world.

ACTIVITY 7

Escher-like Tessellations

The Dutch artist M. C. Escher often used tessellating figures in his artwork. Although the Islamic tessellations that Escher studied did not include human or animal figures, Escher is known for his creation of animal tessellations. His technique was based on the geometry of simple tessellating shapes like the quadrilateral, the triangle, and the regular hexagon and involved "carving" new shapes from these simple polygons. His tessellations are formed by altering the shape of one side of a polygon and then adding the same shape in a rotated or translated form to another side of the polygon. These two steps allowed the shapes to tessellate, or "fit" into each other to tile the plane.

You can create your own Escher-type tessellations by following the diagrams shown below.

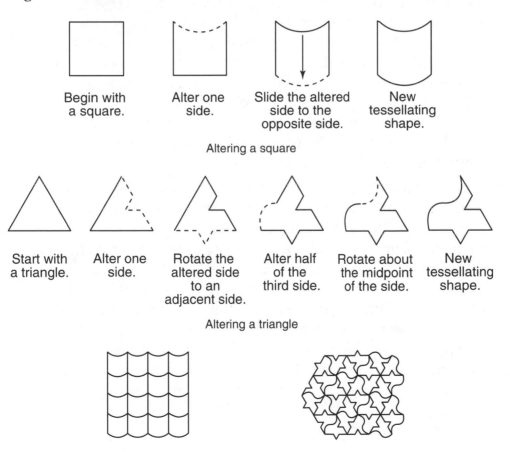

Begin with a square.   Alter one side.   Slide the altered side to the opposite side.   New tessellating shape.

Altering a square

Start with a triangle.   Alter one side.   Rotate the altered side to an adjacent side.   Alter half of the third side.   Rotate about the midpoint of the side.   New tessellating shape.

Altering a triangle

The altered-square tessellation   The altered-triangle tessellation

ACTIVITY 8

Tiles, Quasi-Crystals, and Staircases

1. Investigate the Golden Triangle and its relationship to Penrose tiles. Jay Kappraff's book *Connections* may be helpful in finding information on this topic.

2. Mathematicians are investigating whether a set of tiles exists that tessellates aperiodically and bears no relationship to the Golden Ratio. They suspect that none do, but they have yet to prove it. Find recent articles on this topic, and report on your findings.

3. Penrose had a knack for playing tricks with geometry. When he was young, he and his father drew the "Penrose staircase," the impossible staircase that we see in Escher's work. The staircase spirals up and down without going anywhere. Escher's *Ascending and Descending* shows a line of men proceeding upwards and downwards at the same time. Escher's work is filled with paradoxes, that is, self-contradictory ideas or seemingly impossible situations. See if you can find some other examples of paradoxes in Escher's works. Also, investigate the Penrose triangle, which demonstrates the paradox of seeing a two-dimensional drawing of an object that cannot be created in three dimensions.

4. Robert Ammann, a recreational mathematician, has discovered some interesting properties of Penrose tilings. Ammann explored the spacing between the tiles using a pentagonal grid in which the lines are not perpendicular, unlike in the Cartesian coordinate graph grid. Ammann invented a grid with five intersecting lines, each set 72° from the next, producing a grid with five-fold symmetry. The tricky part was drawing the grid over the tiles so that each line passed through each and every tile. Quite cleverly, Ammann discovered that if he altered the distances between the lines, the grid would work. The distance between the

An "Ammann line" is one of two lengths—either a longer length a or a shorter length b. The ratio of the longer length to the shorter length is the Golden Ratio! Do some research on Ammann lines. Create an illustration demonstrating his ideas, and show that the ratio of the distances between the grid lines is indeed the Golden Ratio.

Graphing Calculator Explorations

Using dynamic geometry software, experiment with translating, rotating, dilating, and reflecting drawn objects. Try to create shapes that tessellate.

ACTIVITY 10

Internet Explorations

1. This Web site gives a thorough introduction to hyperbolic geometry and also provides the full NonEuclid software for Win95, Win3.x, and Macintosh:

   `http://cs.unm.edu/~joel/NonEuclid/`

   NonEuclid is a software simulation offering straightedge-and-compass constructions in hyperbolic geometry— a geometry of Einstein's general relativity theory and curved hyperspace.

2. These Web sites provide information and ideas related to Penrose tiles:

   `http://www.sciencenews.org/sn_arch/10_12_96/bob1.html`

   `http://galaxy.cau.edu/tsmith/kw/goldenpenrose.html`

The Tessellating Tetrominoes Quilt

The pattern for the Tessellating Tetrominoes quilt was inspired by the computer game Tetris™, which is based on the tiling pattern of tetrominoes, shapes made by joining four congruent squares with their sides adjacent. The rotations and translations require a two-dimensional plane. The reflection requires a three-dimensional space for the transformation, because the "flip" requires lifting the shape off the plane and repositioning it in its reflected or mirror-image form. The two-dimensional screen would not allow "flips" for the computer game, so two additional shapes—the reflected Z and L—were added. Because not all tetrominoes tessellate themselves or one another, the challenge of the game is to visually identify which pieces will "fit" into the open spaces at the bottom of the screen and anticipate their placement as soon as they appear at the top of the screen.

The pattern for the Tessellating Tetrominoes quilt was formed by playing a game of Tetris™ on graph paper instead of a computer. You can develop strategies for certain pieces and prepare surfaces in anticipation of the shapes to come. The quilt designer colored and numbered each of the seven shapes from 1 to 7, and then used the random number generator on a calculator to determine the order of their selection. The shapes were then slid and rotated and moved into position on a 10 × 20 grid similar to the computer screen for the game. Because the quilt design was created on graph paper, there was no time limit, unlike in the computer game. However, the placement of the pieces required the same visual skills and strategies. In this case, the quilt became an artistic legacy of an enjoyable experience.

Designing Your Quilt

Follow these steps to create your design:

Step 1   Simulate a game of Tetris™ using a random number generator, and place the pieces on a 10 × 20 grid to create your design.

Step 2   Select seven colors for the seven tetromino shapes, and color your quilt design.

Mathematical Quilts—No Sewing Required!
©1999 Key Curriculum Press

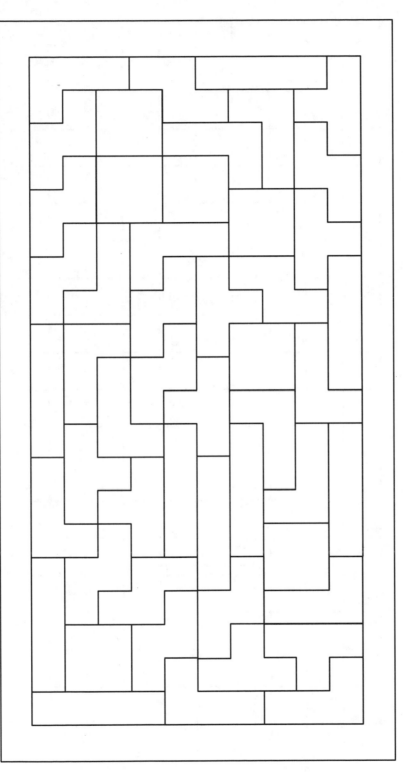

Making the Tessellating Tetrominoes Quilt

The Tessellating Tetrominoes quilt was constructed of cotton fabric in seven colors. You will need $\frac{1}{4}$ yard of each color fabric. The colors were selected to match the colors in the actual computer game. The design drafted on a 10×20 grid of squares on graph paper, based on playing the Tetris game, and then the pattern was colored in as a guide for fabric placement.

Rather than cutting fabric pieces in the shape of the tetrominoes, the designer drafted and pieced this quilt as 200 individual squares. The irregular forms of the tetrominoes make stitching them together awkward, if not impossible. The unit of measure for the individual squares is $1\frac{1}{2}$ inches. Allowing for a $\frac{1}{4}$-inch seam on each side, cut each square 2 inches on a side. To determine the number of squares needed for each color, count the number of pieces of each color and multiply by 4.

Lay out the 200 pieces of the quilt design in grid form on a large surface. Use the drafted version of the quilt as a guide for color placement. Sew the vertical seams for each row, and press the seams to one side. If you press the seams in row 1 to the left, then press the seams in row 2 to the right. Continue this alternating pattern of pressing the seams.

Sew the rows together in a similar process. Stitch row 1 to row 2, carefully matching the seams and using the alternating directions of the pressed seams to align the junctions perfectly. Tear out and restitch any junction that does not align correctly. Stitch rows 3 and 4 the same way, then rows 5 and 6, and so on, finishing with rows 19 and 20. Press the horizontal seams downward. Continue this process, joining these two-row sections, pressing, and then joining the four-row sections, until the quilt is completed. Add a border to the perimeter of the quilt if you wish.

Insert a lightweight batting between the quilt top and the backing, and baste the three layers together. The original quilt was constructed by machine-quilting along the seams of the tetromino pieces, so the back of the quilt outlined the tetrominoes used for this game. After quilting the outline of the pieces, a $\frac{1}{8}$-inch black ribbon was glued along the seams, outlining the tetrominoes. This technique was used instead of satin stitching because of the bulk of the fabric. It also made it possible to see the entire quilt as pieces of ribbon were glued, which helped to keep the lines straight, and the ribbon also covered some uneven seams. Finally, the quilt was bound with border fabric and a rod pocket was added to the back of the quilt for hanging.

Mathematical Quilts—No Sewing Required!
©1999 Key Curriculum Press

The Penrose Tiles Quilt

The only regular polygons that cover a plane completely are the equilateral triangle, the square, and the regular hexagon. By combining two or more tiles with the additional requirement that the same combination of polygons meet at each vertex, there are eight possible patterns. Three of these patterns are shown below.

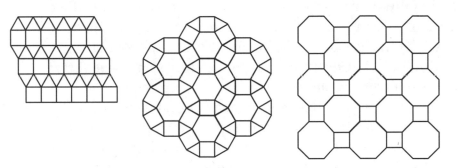

These tiling patterns are periodic—that is, they cover the plane in a repeating pattern, or one that has translational symmetry. A Penrose tiling will cover the plane completely, but it is aperiodic because it does not have translational symmetry.

With each set of Penrose tiles, there are seven possible vertex nets.

Vertex nets for set 1

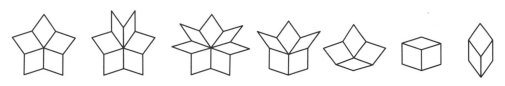

Vertex nets for set 2

The second set of Penrose tiles for the design of this quilt. The "center" of this design is a net of "fat" rhombuses. Once the center was defined, the goal was to cover the flat surface completely. When designing your own quilt, you will probably want to experiment and create your own design rather than trying to duplicate the design in this quilt.

Designing Your Quilt

You can choose either set of Penrose tiles for your quilt design, but do not mix tiles from the different sets. In each case, the "center" of the design must be a vertex net with five-fold symmetry. (Five-fold symmetry means that if you rotate the piece about the center point, it will be in the same position as where you began after each rotation of 72°.) Continue adding tiles forming other vertex nets until you have completely covered your surface.

One way to create your design is to draw it on tracing paper, sliding and rotating the paper to trace each new piece. Another method would be to cut out tagboard templates that you can trace around. For either of these methods, use the patterns on the Penrose Tiles Template Worksheet to draw the tiles. Be sure to match the arcs for the set 1 tiles and the arrows for the set 2 tiles. If you like, you can reduce or enlarge these patterns on a copy machine before you begin.

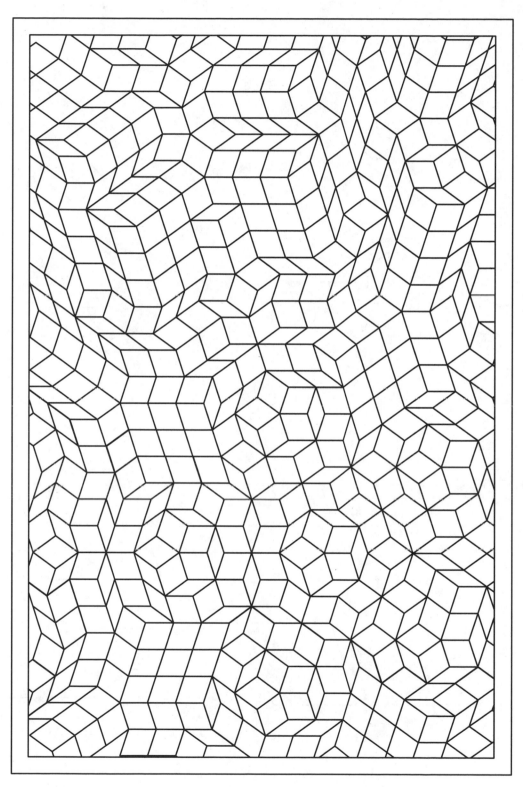

Set 1

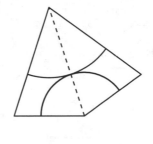
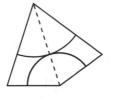
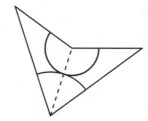

Set 2

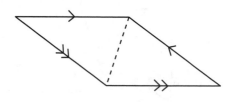
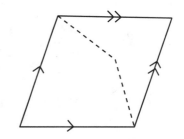

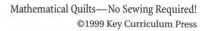

Making the Penrose Tiles Quilt

The size of this quilt is 37″ × 56″. The backing requires 2 yards of fabric. Because this quilt is quite large, you will need to use a very firm batting. You will find it helpful if you choose a thin cotton fabric, because the "skinny" rhombuses are difficult to work with. This quilt is a "partner" to the Fibonacci Sequence and the Golden Rectangle quilt in that the leftover 55 colors used in that quilt were enough to complete the Penrose Tiles quilt.

Design the quilt on freezer paper first. The freezer paper will help keep the design "squared up." When your design is completed, arrange colored rhombuses over the design to see what the overall effect will be. Even though the angles in this design are unusual ones, the original quilt was pieced completely on a sewing machine.

Begin the piecing at the very center of the star. Next, lay rhombuses next to the star and continue piecing. As you add each additional "ring" of rhombuses, pressing becomes more important. Because you are sewing in a circular fashion, you may have to resew an occasional seam to keep the quilt "flat."

The binding on this quilt is fairly wide. Because of the varied amounts of tension along the edge of the quilt, the binding was not cut on the bias. To help the quilt hang flat, tubes were sewn to both the top and bottom edges.

The Poincaré Plane Quilt

The design for this quilt was based on a P6 base group symmetry. This means that once the motif is established, in this case one-sixth of the circle, the motif is repeated after a rotation of 60°.

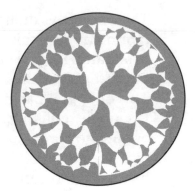

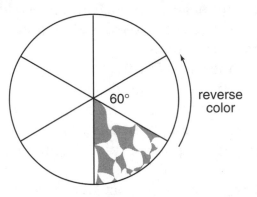

For this quilt, the designer decided to tessellate the Poincaré plane with quadrilaterals. As you may notice, the tile used in this quilt does not have mirror symmetry. In other words, there is no axis of symmetry. Instead, rotations were used to create the tile. Notice that when a side was altered, this alteration was rotated to the adjacent side of the tile.

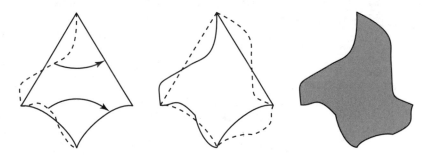

We designed the smaller tiles individually, keeping in mind the overall design of the larger tile.

Mathematical Quilts—No Sewing Required!
©1999 Key Curriculum Press

Designing Your Quilt

Before starting your quilt design, you might want to enlarge the pattern for the Poincaré plane. You can do this on a photocopier or by hand. Here are two methods for designing your quilt:

1. You can create your design on the Poincaré plane design template, drawing the design in each of the six sections of the plane. Follow these steps to create your design.

   Step 1 Choose a section of the plane that is one-sixth of the entire circle. Design a tile to fit the largest section closest to the center of the quilt.

   Step 2 After this tile is completed, move out from the center and draw a "smaller" tiling pattern in the next region. The shape of the tile used should be similar to the tile in step 1.

   Step 3 Again moving outward, draw the smaller and smaller tiling patterns, keeping each tile shape similar to the original figure.

   Step 4 Color your tiling design.

   Step 5 Rotate the design 60°, and repeat the outline of the figures, reversing the colors as you work.

   Step 6 Repeat step 5 four more times until the design is complete.

2. Follow steps 1–4, drawing your design in the Poincaré plane 60° wedge template. Make six copies of your design on a photocopier. Cut out the six wedges, arrange the pieces around a point, and glue them to a large piece of paper to see your complete design.

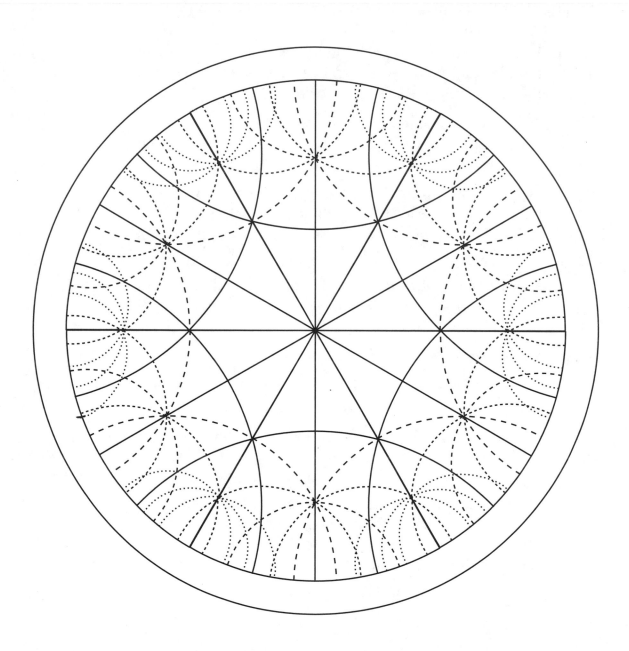

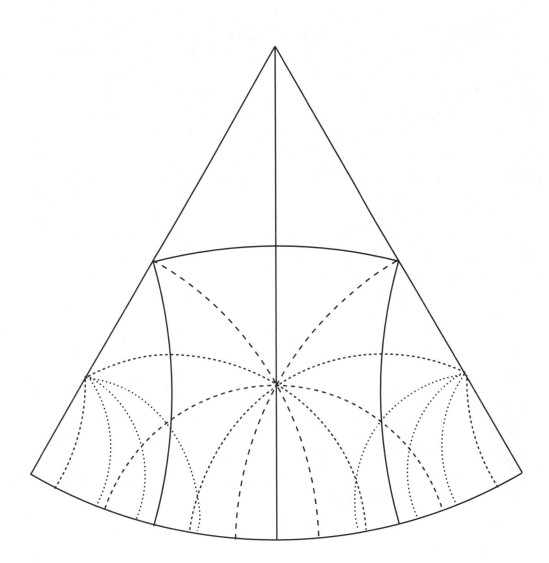

Making the Poincaré Plane Quilt

This quilt is 44 inches in diameter. You will need 1 yard of fabric for the backing, 1 yard of fabric for the background, and $1\frac{1}{2}$ yards of a contrasting fabric for the design and the border. The border for the original quilt was made by cutting bias strips out of the matching blue material used for the birdlike figures.

Before starting your quilt, enlarge your Poincaré plane to the desired size on freezer paper, drawing on the dull side of the paper. Once you have enlarged the plane, choose a section that is one-sixth of the entire circle. Design a tile to fit the largest section closest to the center of the quilt. After you complete this section, begin drawing the "smaller" tilings adjacent to the larger one. Again working outward, draw the smallest tilings, keeping each tile shape similar to the original figures. Color this section on the freezer paper. Rotate the design 60°, and repeat the outline of the figures, reversing the colors as you work. Repeat this process four more times until the design is complete.

An appliqué technique was used to sew this quilt. Use fusible interfacing to keep the pieces in place. It is important that you continue pressing as you work.

After you insert the batting between the top and the backing, outline the figures with machine quilting. Also quilt the areas to indicate wings and eyes. Sew the bias binding to the front side of the quilt along the outside edge of the quilt, and then hand-stitch the binding to the back of the quilt, turning the seam allowance under as you work. Cut a circular frame out of pegboard, and glue 1-inch-wide Velcro™ to the perimeter of the board using epoxy glue. Sew Velcro™ to the back side of the quilt. For a smaller quilt, you may not need the pegboard support.

Mathematical Quilts—No Sewing Required!
©1999 Key Curriculum Press

The activities in this section are good extensions for transformational geometry. Students at all levels can benefit from practice with "motion geometry," using either the formal terms for transformations (translations, reflections, rotations) or the informal terms (flips, slides, turns). Activities in which students move geometric shapes around the plane and have both a tactile and visual experience can improve their visualization and strategic thinking skills and prepare them for the study of formal geometry.

In Activity 1, students determine whether all triangles and quadrilaterals will tessellate the plane. In Activities 2 and 3, they are introduced to polyominoes and some polyomino puzzles. The activities for the Tessellating Tetrominoes quilt also involve an exploration of symmetry and manipulation of various tetromino shapes. Encourage students to make tagboard or plastic templates so that they can manipulate the shapes. They can also generate these shapes and move them about on a computer, and then transfer their designs from the screen to paper.

Students will enjoy creating designs with the various polyomino shapes. Keep a supply of dot paper handy so that they will be encouraged to explore beyond the activities. If the computer game Tetris™ is available, let students play it to reinforce the idea of tessellating figures with the added skills of hand-eye coordination between the screen and the joystick/mouse as they move the shapes into place before they fall to the bottom of the screen. Students will enjoy developing and discussing strategies for placing the pieces. For example, the "O" shape requires two level squares upon which to land. Students must devise a strategy for keeping two level spaces open for both this shape and others with the same requirement. These are higher-level thinking skills.

The activities related to the Penrose Tiles quilt introduce students to the concept of aperiodic tilings. In Activity 4, students find all of the vertex nets for each set of Penrose tiles. This activity provides a good opportunity to discuss various kinds of symmetry. Some of the vertex nets have five-fold rotational symmetry while others have bilateral symmetry. In Activity 5, students explore a special relationship between pentagons and the ratio of the areas in a set of tiles.

In Activity 6, students explore some properties of non-Euclidean geometry, particularly those related to the Poincaré plane. You could suggest that they read Edward Abbot's *Flatland* to see what is meant by describing life in a different geometry environment. Read some excerpts from the book to encourage students to explore these ideas and to expose them to the idea of creative writing in mathematics.

The artwork of M. C. Escher provides examples of tessellations that are created from complex shapes formed by "carving" simpler shapes. Activity 7 encourages students to create their own Escher-type shapes to tessellate the plane. As they create their shapes, students will have to problem solve and do strategic planning. This activity often results in unusually creative projects from students. They enjoy the challenge of creating their own unique tile.

In Activity 8, students do independent research related to key mathematical concepts to broaden their understanding.

For the quilt designs in this section, students should be encouraged to create their own unique designs rather than trying to replicate the designs in the quilts pictured. It is much more fun to experiment and come up with individual creations, and students will probably find it quite tedious trying to reproduce the quilt designs shown.

Answers and Comments

Activity 1

Any triangle will tessellate the plane because the sum of the angles in a triangle is 180°, which is a factor of 360°. Any quadrilateral will tessellate the plane because the sum of the angles in a quadrilateral is 360°.

Activity 2

1. There are one monomino, one domino, and two tromino tiles.

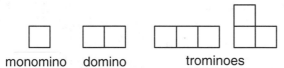

monomino   domino   trominoes

2. a. There are five tetromino shapes.

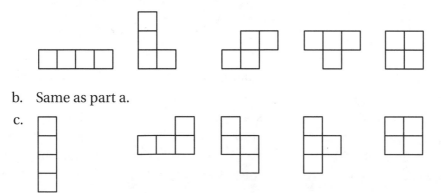

b. Same as part a.

c.

Mathematical Quilts—No Sewing Required!
©1999 Key Curriculum Press

d.

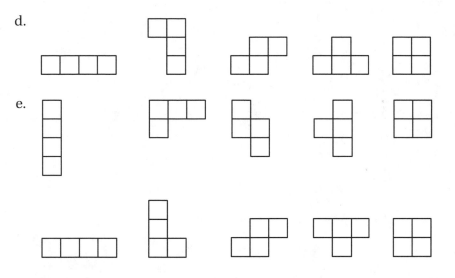

e.

f. Answers may vary. Students likely will find it most difficult to rotate the L and the Z.

g. The two pieces that had to be added were a reflected L and a reflected Z.

Activity 3

1. Each of the tetromino shapes will tessellate the plane.

2. Answers will vary.

3.

4.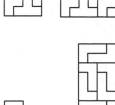

Activity 4

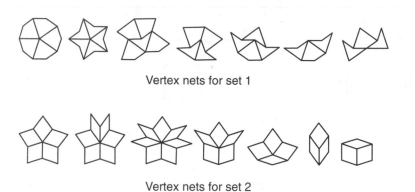

Vertex nets for set 1

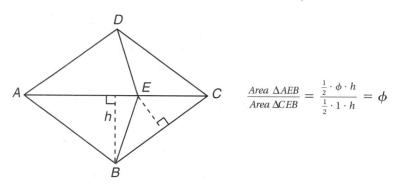

Vertex nets for set 2

Activity 5

The ratio of the areas in each case is the Golden Ratio. One way to show this is to consider the Penrose rhombus in which $AE = \phi$ and $EC = 1$.

$$\frac{Area\ \triangle AEB}{Area\ \triangle CEB} = \frac{\frac{1}{2} \cdot \phi \cdot h}{\frac{1}{2} \cdot 1 \cdot h} = \phi$$

Activity 6

Answers will vary. To help students visualize what this world is like, you might want to list the various theorems, postulates, and properties of Euclidean and hyperbolic geometry and compare and contrast each category. This model gives students a chance to experience another geometry without leaving the confines of a secure Euclidean world.

Activity 7

Answers will vary. There are many sources available that provide student tessellation activities.

Activity 8

Answers will vary.

Activity 9

Answers will vary.

Activity 10

There are no "answers" for this activity.

TEACHER NOTES

Resources and Selected Readings

Boles, Martha, and Rochelle Newman. *Universal Patterns,* Books 1 and 2. Bradford, MA: Pythagorean Press, 1990, 1992.

Devlin, Keith. *Mathematics: The Science of Patterns.* New York: Freeman, 1997.

Eightysomething! The Newsletter for Users of TI Graphing Calculators. Vol. 6, No. 3, Spring 1997.

Emmer, Michele, ed. *The Visual Mind: Art and Mathematics.* Cambridge, MA: MIT Press, 1993.

Gardner, Martin. *Penrose Tiles to Trapdoor Ciphers.* New York: Freeman, 1989.

Kappraff, Jay. *Connections: The Geometric Bridge Between Art and Science.* New York: McGraw-Hill, 1991.

Martin, George E. *Polyominoes: A Guide to Puzzles and Problems in Tiling.* Washington, D.C.: The Mathematical Association of America: 1991.

O'Daffer, Phares G., and Stanley R. Clemens. *Geometry: An Investigative Approach,* 2d ed. Reading, MA: Addison-Wesley, 1992.

Pappas, Theoni. *Mathematics Appreciation.* San Carlos, CA: Wide World Publishing/Tetra, 1986.

Pedoe, Dan. *Geometry and the Visual Arts.* New York: Dover, 1976.

Seymour, Dale, and Jill Britton. *Introduction to Tessellations.* Palo Alto, CA: Dale Seymour Publications, 1989.

Von Baeyer, Hans C. "Impossible Crystals." *Discover,* New York: February 1990.

Wolfe, Harold E. *Non-Euclidean Geometry.* New York: Holt, Rinehart & Winston, 1945.

The following articles will be of interest, as they expand on some of the ideas presented in this section. They are from *The Visual Mind,* edited by Michelle Emmer. The articles include "New Representative Methods for Real and Imaginary Environments," by Emilio Frisia, pages 249–56; "The Geometries Behind My Spherical Paintings," by Dick Termes, pages 243–48; "Compound Tilings and Perfect Colourings," by J. F. Rigby, pages 177–86; and "Automatic Generation of Hyperbolic Tilings," by Silvio Levy, pages 165–70.

1-Centimeter Dot Paper

$\frac{1}{4}$-Inch Dot Paper

1-Centimeter Grid Paper

$\frac{1}{4}$-Inch Grid Paper

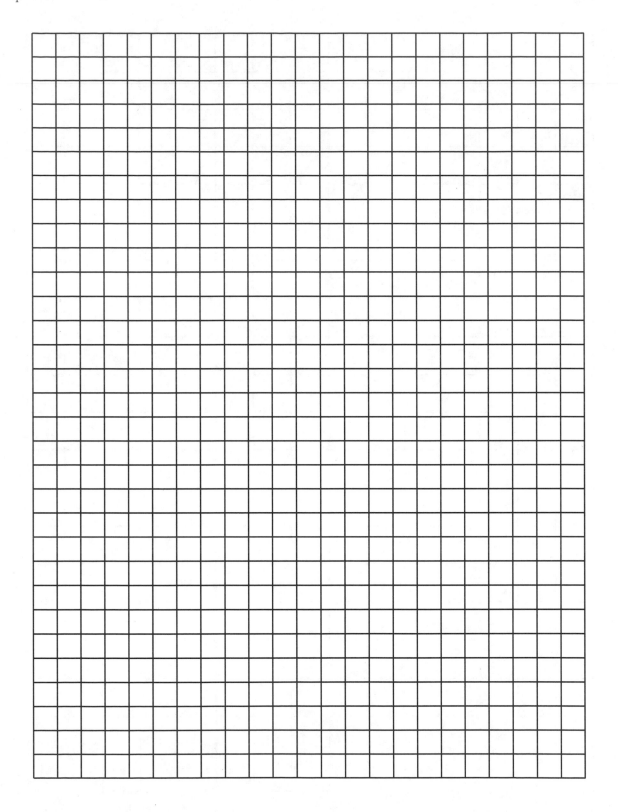